FALLING INTO THE RHYTHM OF *Life*

What People Are Saying About
FALLING INTO THE RHYTHM OF *Life*

"Sharon's tenacity and passion shine through as she rediscovers herself after a terrifying experience. Sharon has learned through her time with horses a unique wisdom as she shares *Life Lessons Straight from the Horse's Mouth*": *powerful tips full of simple and easy ways to live with focus and purpose.*"

—**Wendy Golding**, The Horse Spirit Connections FEEL (Facilitated Equine Experiential Learning) Program

"Sharon Campbell Rayment has knocked it out of the park with *Falling into the Rhythm of Life*. It's loaded with inspiring life principles that enable you to overcome any challenge or setback, so you can become the greatest version of yourself. Her insights and wisdom are absolute gems!"

— **Jayne Blumenthal**, The 7-Figure Mindset Mentor

"If you or someone you love has suffered a serious setback, you've got to keep Falling into the Rhythm of Life within arm's reach. It equips you with energizing principles that empower you to flow through any challenge with ease and optimism."

—**Judy O'Beirn**, Hasmark Publishing, Best Selling Author of Unwavering Strength Series

"The only thing as amazing as Sharon Campbell Rayment's inspiring story is the incredible lessons and principles she shares in, *Falling into the Rhythm of Life*. If you've ever suffered a setback and have struggled to get through it, this is the book you absolutely must read!"

—**Steve Lowell**, International Professional Speaker and Mentor to Speakers Worldwide

FALLING
INTO THE
RHYTHM
OF
Life

*Life Lessons Straight from
the Horse's Mouth*

SHARON CAMPBELL-RAYMENT

New York

FALLING INTO THE RHYTHM OF *Life*
Life Lessons Straight from the Horse's Mouth

Published in New York, New York, by Morgan James Publishing. Morgan James and The Entrepreneurial Publisher are trademarks of Morgan James, LLC.
www.MorganJamesPublishing.com

The Morgan James Speakers Group can bring authors to your live event. For more information or to book an event visit The Morgan James Speakers Group at www.TheMorganJamesSpeakersGroup.com.

Shelfie

A free eBook edition is available
with the purchase of this print book.

CLEARLY PRINT YOUR NAME ABOVE IN UPPER CASE

Instructions to claim your free eBook edition:
1. Download the Shelfie app for Android or iOS
2. Write your name in **UPPER CASE** above
3. Use the Shelfie app to submit a photo
4. Download your eBook to any device

ISBN 978-1-61448-835-4 paperback
ISBN 978-1-61448-836-1 eBook
ISBN 978-1-61448-837-8 hardcover
Library of Congress Control Number:
2015912977

Cover Design by:
Rachel Lopez
www.r2cdesign.com

Interior Design by:
Bonnie Bushman
The Whole Caboodle Graphic Design

Morgan James The Entrepreneurial Publisher™

Builds

with...

Habitat for Humanity®
Peninsula and
Greater Williamsburg

In an effort to support local communities, raise awareness and funds, Morgan James Publishing donates a percentage of all book sales for the life of each book to Habitat for Humanity Peninsula and Greater Williamsburg.

Get involved today! Visit
www.MorganJamesBuilds.com

DEDICATION

I dedicate this to my husband Doug with love and gratitude for standing beside me throughout this journey and accepting me completely as I AM!

I share this with great love to my daughters, Megan and Mikayla.

And of course, to Malachi, the messenger of God, who truly lived up to his name.

CONTENTS

ACKNOWLEDGMENTS

A great story does not happen in isolation. God's grace brings people into your life as it unfolds to offer support, love, inspiration, wisdom, joy, and healing. The list of people who should be acknowledged here is long so please know that I extend sincere thanks to all who have entered my life even for a brief time in this journey.

First and foremost I must acknowledge God's unwavering presence in my life and His messenger Malachi. As the saying goes, God always arrives on time for the messages we are ready to receive. If I would not slow down, I would have to fall down to understand that life is about authentic presence and love. Life's lessons become easier when all you can do is be in the presence of horses and listen to the rhythm of life.

I give special thanks to my husband Doug and our girls for continuing this journey together with all of the bucks, twists, and spins through life balanced with joy, hope, and unconditional love. And of course for tolerating the innumerable questions and the time it takes for me to explain to people why I have the accent! As our favourite song by Alan Jackson "Remember When" reminds us—life was changed, disassembled, and rearranged but we danced through week to week and we never gave up! Here's to many more years of dancing.

When life knocks you down you truly find the friends that are angels to lift you up and carry you. If one tear fell from my eyes I knew my friend Lana would be walking through the door. A friend, a mum, and cohort in adventures that led to hours of laughter and breathtaking moments flying through the bush with Brad and Bill! Thank you with all of my heart.

Great thanks to Peggy McColl for the patience it has taken to work with me over the last few years. It may have taken me twice as long perhaps than some of your other clients, but I've loved the journey and the friendship we have created along the way.

I am also thankful to Judy O'Beirn for the calls, the friendship, and the amazing insight and inspirational visit with my horses.

Thank you to Wendy and Andre of Horse Spirit Connections for taking the time to share and teach the unique way of working with the spirit of the horses and the awakening of intuition within my heart.

I also wish to thank Steve Lowell for helping me craft a wonderful Keynote presentation that inspires and uplifts others to get "back up on the horse again" when life knocks them down.

And I give thanks to Jayne Blumenthal who, if it were not for her, this book and all of the daily tasks and checklists would never have been done. Thanks Jayne for helping me make decisions and following through and to make lists and to git 'er done!

And to everyone at Morgan James Publishing great thanks for making this book a reality and a great success!

Thanks so much to Phil Marks for editing the manuscript. You certainly made it an easy read by rearranging many of my thoughts and

I so enjoyed the wee anecdotes you shared along the way. Also to Ginger Marks of DocUmeant Designs for preparing the book for Morgan James!

Life really is an AND … we are not limited in any way because loving makes it so.

AND so it is!

FALLING INTO
THE RHYTHM OF LIFE
Foreword by Peggy McColl

Every person goes through challenging times in his or her life. Sometimes the challenges are more difficult than others, but nonetheless, challenges (or sometimes known as "adversity") do happen—and they never seem to happen at a good time.

In her compelling book, *Falling into the Rhythm of Life,* Sharon Campbell Rayment shares her moving story of adversity and triumph. You'll learn that it isn't about getting knocked down in life, it's about what you do when it happens.

After a terrible fall from her horse, Sharon, not only rebuilt her life, but she made a decision to share the most powerful lessons of her own experience with others through speaking engagements, workshops, her retreat center and the empowering stories in this fabulous book.

I have been a good friend and mentor to Sharon for several years. After her tragic accident I have seen her go from being only able to speak on the phone for five to 10 minutes, to being able to enthrall large audiences with inspiring presentations on how to overcome any challenge and transform your life.

Even more impressive is how through her speaking and her horses at her retreat, she has been able to uplift and change the lives of so many others who experienced traumatic life-changing events.

Falling into the Rhythm of Life shares Sharon's remarkable story of healing, while providing proven strategies you can use to overcome despair and find a powerful new life purpose.

I have read hundreds of books and written a dozen of them myself, but I have never read a book quite like this one. The thing I especially love about Sharon's book is that she shares her journey with you and captivates you right from the first line of the book, and keeps you engaged through the very last word.

She also has a wonderful sense of humor that I am certain you are going to love. As you sit down with, *Falling into the Rhythm of Life*, be sure to give yourself the uninterrupted time to go through the entire book. It isn't essential that you complete the book in one sitting—but I know you will find it difficult to stop and set it aside.

Falling into the Rhythm of Life is filled with some of the most powerful messages you will ever read. At the end of the book you will find the messages of Malachi. The messages of Malachi are brilliant, thought provoking, and they have the potential to truly change your life in glorious ways.

I encourage you to enjoy this magnificent book and put its empowering lessons into practice in your life today. And, be sure to get an extra copy for someone you love. I am certain it will enable them to gain newfound inner strength, and navigate emotionally difficult times with confidence, grace and dignity.

Chapter 1

THE GREAT FALL

Have you ever done something—in a single moment—that changed your life forever?

I have.

And it's a moment I will never forget.

*I*t happened on July 11, 2008 during a performance I put on for the families of the children who had participated in a weeklong horseback riding camp at my farm in Ontario, Canada. My decision to not wear a helmet while riding resulted in the death of my former self.

I began running these camps because although I was working full time as a minister in three churches, I felt that I should fill my summers with more activity so why not book every week with kids for camps. I mean really—I had a whole month off so why wouldn't I fill it with more work rather than hanging by the pool with the kids and relaxing! There it is—number one clue that I was a workaholic. I could never rest nor stop trying to take on more work.

We had horses on our farm because we had started horseback riding lessons to help me get away from the pull of the fitness club I owned at that time just prior to going into ministry. So it seems that maybe I tended to do too many things at once. I opened my fitness club while I was still a public health nurse and since I was on maternity leave at the time, why not open a fitness club? Honestly? Who in their right mind believes they can run a fitness club, work full time as a public health nurse, and have a newborn to care for? Well evidently I thought this was a good idea! Just to give you a heads up—NOT a great idea! Maternity leave is not a vacation!

I remember calling my mom on a particular day that life was out of control as I tried to balance everything. My babysitter had called in sick so I had to stay home with my daughter Megan. I received an inappropriate and nasty call from a member of my club and immediately after talking to her I picked up the phone to talk to my mom and of course broke down crying. She encouraged me to pack up Megan and come for a visit. Mom of course knew how stressed I had become and she asked me, "Sharon is it money that you are worried about?" And of course I replied, "Yes." And she gave me the greatest counsel of my 30 years as her daughter. "Do not ever put money before family and friends." But I told her, "Money isn't everything, but when you don't have it you feel like you are struggling for oxygen. You really can't do without it." She advised me to let the job as a public health nurse go if running the fitness club was my true desire and to trust that with the extra energy and focus this would allow me to run the fitness club successfully. This way, my family would have me home and available, not just physically, but mentally as well. You see, often when I was home I was thinking of work and when at work I was thinking of home. I was trapped in a maze of thoughts that left my family very little of me emotionally, mentally, and physically.

It was when I was in the fitness industry that I felt called to ministry. This was only six months after I had opened the fitness club, which had been my dream since I was fifteen. It was only a week after the heart-to-heart talk I had with my mom that she died suddenly of lobar pneumonia. Now, for someone who ran a tight ship and controlled everything down to the smallest detail, I was shocked to feel this loss so suddenly and there was nothing I could do. I remember my dad's call and the confusion, anxiety, and fear that entered my body. As I recall this, it was exactly how I felt after my horseback riding accident.

This led me on a quest to discover the answers to the questions that arose with her loss. How could this have happened? What do I really believe in? Is there a heaven? Will we truly meet again? I began a Masters in Divinity to assist me with these answers, yet as you likely already realize, it only led me to more questions. I can however say that I did find a deep belief and faith within me that I now share with others. I always thought that would be from a church pulpit preaching, which it was for a time, but eventually my greatest call to ministry came from a herd of horses after a life altering accident.

My father passed away in 1999, six years after my mom. Doug and I now had two daughters, Megan who was seven, and Mikayla who was four when we moved into my parent's home. It was strange at first. Doug was working at a job that involved working night shifts, and the first evening in the house he was on the midnight shift. It was strange lying in bed in the room where both of my parents had died. Mom had died suddenly and dad after a battle with cancer. Yet as I lay there I did a flop and drop of my bible, which always seems to speak to me, and I read Psalm 4, "I will both lie down and sleep in peace; for you alone, O Lord, make me lie down in safety."[1] That peace that surpasses all understanding entered into my soul and I escaped to the peace of sleep.

---

1   The Holy Bible, New Revised Standard Version, Anglicized Edition, Oxford University Press 1998.

As I mentioned earlier, I loved to work. I was a workaholic. My husband's motto is "Work to live" and mine "Live to work!" I found it difficult to relax so we took an acre of "good corn land" as my dad would call it and turned it into a large garden with a gazebo, pond, lovely trees, and a 52-foot labyrinth. A labyrinth is a walking path, meditation in motion I call it. The path helps you to focus, centre, release stress, and pause for a few minutes in your busy life. I had been trained by Dr. Rev. Lauren Artress to facilitate labyrinth walks so it seemed appropriate that we would put one in our garden area behind the huge equipment shed we had on our farm. As you can see, "Go big or go home." was my motto. If you are going to do something, do it right and make it worthwhile.

And so we converted a few acres of our farmland into a retreat area for folks to pause and pray. We also added horse stalls within the equipment shed and started to renovate an area inside for bathrooms and a meeting area. It felt right that this would be shared with children who wanted to be on the farm and near horses. My theme was from Kevin Costner's movie *Field of Dreams*, "Build it and they will come!"

We also ran camps for children with special needs. During Christmas of 2006 Cindy, a director of a special needs riding program, approached me. She asked if I would be interested in running horseback riding camps with her for special population children as part of the City of Chatham program. As I was working full time in ministry, and still going to school for my master's program, Doug and I had decided a few days before her call that we would shut down the camps so I could focus on my ministry. Cindy did not accept "no" for an answer however, and in January of 2007 she called again and asked if I could come in to visit her and we could discuss this. I knew that if I went in to talk with her that I would say "yes" but I still went in and yes—I did agree to hold the summer camps.

So every summer we ran five to six weeks of camp for general population children and a few weeks for special population children with ADHD, Down's syndrome, autism, and physical handicaps. I must admit, the weeks with the children with the special needs were always my favorites and my staff's favorite as well. And after I say this I think of the other kids that came through my camps and I can say that each was wonderful and grand for there is a special magic that happens when children and horses interact. To allow for these extra camps I would have to expand our operation. In the spring of 2008, after completing my Masters in Divinity in December of 2007, we added additional stalls to our barn, put up an inside riding area—a MegaDome, which was 132 feet long and 60 feet wide to accommodate the kids when it rained and I had planned to do riding lessons in the winter as well. I changed our road sign from "Creating Harmony Spirit Centre" to "Camp Achieve" and bought three additional horses. Two of which I purchased and brought home without my husband knowing.

Well, let me explain that. First, they are the best pulling team I have ever owned, which by the way, I had no idea how to drive a team of horses nor owned any previously, but regardless of that, to the farm they came. It was a funny God-incident that I met Doug at a cross road on our way to purchase these horses. Doug was in a work truck so I didn't recognize who he was nor did I expect him to be where I was at that time. I said to Lana, my cohort in crime, my daughter, and my friend and employee Jaclyn who were in the truck "Why is that truck waiting so long to turn? Oh well, we'll go anyway." Within seconds my phone rang and it was Doug. "Where are you going?" he asked. "Oh we are just out for a drive." I replied. "Why are you in Highgate?" he inquired. I looked around the cab of the truck at the girls with the expression of "How does he know?" "Oh we were just heading over to look at something at a farm. Just out and about. Nothing really." I tried to state casually and laughed. "Ok" he said tentatively knowing full well there was something up. Yet in our 24 years of marriage he never got too worked up about things, which was a good thing, because off we went to purchase the two Fjord horses, Brad and Bill, two pulling carts, a saddle and a trailer. After our grand adventure I dropped Lana off and when we arrived in our laneway Doug was in the garage. Both Jaclyn and Megan jumped out quickly to avoid any questions from Doug but he immediately knew something was up as he asked "So what did you do today?"

In hindsight he had many reasons to be angry. First the purchase of the horses without his knowledge and second we were out touring when I should have been earning money rather than spending it but it seemed I was driven to do and experience everything I could as fast and furious as I could just before my accident. Nothing was going to stand in my way or hold me back. I worked hard, played hard, and felt the exhilaration of doing more, gaining more, and spending more.

But honestly, all of this had become too much. The renovations to the farm, running lessons at night, working full time at the churches and trying to balance work and home were taking their toll. That spring we had a very challenging time at our churches as we lost a young man suddenly, and in such an unexpected way, that it left the community reeling. It was the hardest funeral I had ever done. The senselessness left me stunned and questioning my beliefs when suddenly one of my beloved church members learned she had liver cancer and passed away a mere three weeks later. Ministers are never to have "favourites" in their church members, but Mildred was one of the most gracious and loving persons I had known. At the end of every service I know she went out of her way to make me feel great. My sermon that Sunday was always the best she had ever heard! The sudden loss of these two people, and an additional member whose granddaughter worked for me at the camp for a number of years left me exhausted—emotionally, mentally, physically, and spiritually drained.

On Sundays, during our pastoral prayer time in our church services, in the silence as we raised to God the names of those that needed guidance, love, grace, and help, I would add my own name. I would pray, "Lord, just let me faint here. Let me have a wee swoon. You know, like the old Southern belles with their corsets too tight. Then people will know that I am tired and worn out and need to rest." Little did I know that this prayer would be answered, but not as a wee swoon, but as "a great fall."

Chapter 2

BE CAREFUL WHAT
YOU WISH FOR

O n July 11, 2008 we were preparing to do an afternoon show for the parents of the children who had attended camp that week. We had 12 girls who had participated and we always worked during the week to put a show together for the parents, siblings, friends, and grandparents of the girls so they could show off their riding skills.

There were the tasks of getting the horses tacked up, setting up chairs for the parents, running lines for music, and setting up barrels and other pieces of equipment to showcase the girls' skills. Jaclyn and I recalled later that we had an odd feeling that day. It was bright and sunny but windy. We both felt fragmented, disorganized, and unprepared but we pressed on through our feelings.

All was ready by one p.m. for the families to see the big show! The kids were divided up into teams and each child rode a horse doing a number of maneuvers that parents cheered and clapped for. And then the last game of the day that was always the most fun was to begin— "The Rubber Ducky Race." My team members would lead the children on their horses from one end of the arena to the other carrying a bucket of water. Their mission was for them to fill the empty bucket at the opposite end of the arena with enough water to make a rubber ducky float above the rim.

After playing a few rounds, I upped the ante (as per usual). I told kids that I would win the race by carrying a bucket of water to the other end of the arena and steer my horse only with a carrot stick (a training tool we use with our horses). So essentially I was hands free!

Even though I had an odd feeling in my gut, I mounted Malachi, grabbed the training stick, and the bucket of water, and took off. But when I got to the other end of the arena, Malachi wouldn't let me get close enough to pour the water from the bucket I was holding into the empty bucket on the barrel. So instead, I turned to go back to the start line, and as I did, the wind blew off my cowboy hat. A scared Malachi took off in a hurry throwing me off balance.

(By the way, it was the first time in seven years that I had not worn a helmet. Up until then, I had always considered myself the "Helmet Queen.")

I tried to regain my balance but was unsuccessful. I remember playing to the crowd to hide my embarrassment that I had become unseated and was losing control. What I should have been doing was comforting Malachi. If I had just reached down to his withers (near the shoulders) and said "Eeeeaaaasssy" slow and kindly he likely would have stopped. He was just frightened, yet my ego took over and I had lost my partnership connection with him. When he turned right to miss the kid's at the finish line, I exited stage left and fell backward.

Falling through the air, I felt weightless and suspended in time. My head slammed off the ground and the force from the bounce—after the first hit—sent my upper body off of the ground only to slam back again a second time hitting my head. It was as if a lightning bolt sent shocks through my body sending a thunderous roar throughout my skull.

Then, I remember darkness—a peaceful midnight black, like a dark velvet curtain—that enveloped me in a cocoon of silent stillness.

Slowly, after what felt like a lifetime had passed, I was drawn out of this dark abyss. I heard a voice calling my name and the sound of people crying. I sensed confusion outside my body, but in my body I was being consumed by shocks of pain shooting through me.

"Why am I here?" I asked.

I heard a voice say, "You have fallen from your horse."

Then, the velvet darkness engulfed me again.

"Why am I here?" I asked a second time.

"You have fallen from your horse," I'm reminded by a patient and soothing voice.

I could only manage to utter the word, "Oh," before the dark curtain fell around me for the third time, and I slipped away from consciousness again.

I traveled in and out of consciousness, confused by two very different worlds that were oddly connected—one draped in velvety darkness and the other surreal and bright.

The next time I opened my eyes I was in the ambulance on my way to the hospital. The hospital visit was a flurry of activity, which I observed as if I were watching a movie of someone else's experience. I joked with the blur of people coming and going as a means of coping with the uncertainty and fear of being strapped to a spinal board in the emergency room. I could do nothing more than stare at the ceiling or at the faces of people streaming in and out of my room.

At one point, as the people talked above me, I remember feeling a "tingling" sensation begin at the crown of my head that descended throughout my entire body. It felt like goose bumps flowing through my body. Slowly it descended throughout my face, down my shoulders, into my chest and back, hips and legs to my feet as if I were being scanned. I tried to express the fear that arose within me, to tell my husband that I was afraid that I was leaving him, that this would be my last moments, but I felt trapped unable to connect to consciousness. It felt as though everyone in the room had left and I was alone. Panic raced through my brain, but this tingling caused my body to feel light, illumined, and beyond the normal weighted feeling I was used to. I knew something was wrong—very wrong. I couldn't speak or move.

I am unsure how long this lasted but as I reconnected to reality again I began to panic. Being unable to move on the backboard frightened me and the pain in my head seemed to be intensified by the inability to move. I remember being able to connect with Doug and he was able to request that I be released from the confines of the straps that held my head in place. Yet this began a new increase in confusion, nausea, dizziness, and pain as the doctor felt my spine, turning me on my side. As the doctor moved inch by inch down the vertebrae I heard her question what the scar on my lower back was. When I was 39 I had back surgery due to a herniated disc and bone spurs that had developed at L4 and L5, which had left me without feeling in my legs and led to emergency surgery. Doug had taken me to University Hospital in London Ontario and after an hour of exams I was told that I would be having back surgery that day. I had observed back surgery when I was a nursing student and it was definitely something I didn't want for myself! I was lying on a stretcher in a busy hallway when I said to Doug "I am not having this surgery. I am getting out of here." Only to be told, "I don't think so. You can't even get up to walk out of here. So you will need to have the surgery."

When asked by the nurse to describe my pain with a number from zero to ten, zero being minimum and ten the worst I had ever felt, I replied jokingly, "Not as bad as child birth!" She was not amused and emphasized that the surgery on my lower spine could remove the pain but I may not regain sensation in my legs. I needed to get serious about this. I wish I had learned from her retort and when I was in the emergency room for my head injury that I didn't automatically cover the pain, fear, and confusion with humour. This humour made the incident seem light and unimportant and Doug later said that although the emergency staff didn't realize it because of my ongoing comedy act, I was not making sense in many of my replies. Yet in the chaos and confusion of the emergency room he remained silent.

Doug is a quiet, thoughtful, and caring person who has always in our 24 years of marriage put his family's needs before his own. His silence to some has been off setting yet beneath the quiet exterior is a man who understands deeply that the important things in life are truly faith, family, and friends. Later he would "circle the wagons", only allowing a limited amount of activity in our home to ensure that I was not overwhelmed by phone calls, tasks, and duties that tired or upset me.

To this day I do not know how he managed this but it only deepened our relationship rather than shatter it as I was truly fragile and felt broken and fragmented into a million pieces like Humpty Dumpty after his fall. It was however, his sense of humour and the conversations we had shared when we met that drew me to him. The funniest moment I can recall is when I had successfully come out of the back surgery yet I was unable to answer the questions the nurses in recovery were asking me. They would ask me my husband's name and I would answer "Bud"—that's my bulldog's name. Later Doug laughed and said when he was allowed into the recovery room and I asked why I was there he was tempted to say to even the score of my inability to recognize him that, "We just had a baby boy." This certainly would have sent me into shock! Thank goodness he held his "revelation" for a later time.

Once again he would stand by a stretcher in a busy emergency area and comfort me. I was disoriented and dizzy, nauseous, and experiencing severe pain from the head injury. The doctors suspected I had suffered a concussion, which is caused by a bump or jolt to the head causing the head to move rapidly back and forth. The concussion does not impact just the area of the head that hit the ground, because the brain is not immobile within the boney skull, it bounces around which can result in bruising in several locations. Later we would discover that it was actually this "contra-coup", the strikes of the brain off the front of the skull that caused the most extensive injury to the left frontal lobe. This bruising can be extensive and lead to a host of post concussive symptoms that are not visible on a CT scan. Nevertheless, to ensure there was not extensive internal bleeding within the brain, I was wheeled to a CT scan. The movement exacerbated the nausea, dizziness, disorientation, headache, and pain I was already experiencing. Conversations and questions echoed in my mind, monitors and alarms rang through my head, and lights stabbed my eyes like knives. I prayed for a quiet place away from the chaos of the emergency room. My prayers were answered when I was discharged from the hospital—without ceremony—within hours.

Doug told me I joked as usual on the way out, embraced Jaclyn, Megan, and my friends Lana and Becky who had waited faithfully (who to this day are friends that stand beside me and know the daily challenges I experience). I asked that my sisters be contacted to let them know what happened and we picked up our usual Friday night pizza.

If Doug and I knew then what we know now I would have rested completely for at least a two-week period after the accident rather than returning to work and all of the sensory exposure I experienced over that first weekend and the following weeks. Concussion awareness and medical prescription for a concussion has changed greatly over the last few years since my accident. Rather than being discharged with the instructions for my husband to "watch me" for the next 24 hours in case the symptoms worsened or I could not be aroused to consciousness from my sleep, I would have been told to isolate myself completely from television, computers, extensive or multiple conversations, reading, bright lights, listening to music, or even talking on the phone. I was given the best instructions at the time however and we were assured that most people start to feel better within a few days. As days turned into weeks, and weeks into months—we would come to realize that this was certainly not the case. Those first 24 hours would evolve into an ongoing and desperate need for support, patience, direction, and compassion as I struggled to cope with the normal activities and interactions of daily life.

I am unsure what happened over that first weekend. As I reflect on this it truly scares me. All of the tasks of running our family, caring for our horses, and watching my condition over the weekend fell to Doug. My daughter Megan, who was 15 at the time, tells me that we slept in my bedroom watching Disney movies over the 2-day weekend. Doug had put a towel over our window to darken the room, as previously, since we lived in the middle of nowhere with the closest neighbours a mile down the road in each direction I had never felt the need for it. But the darkness is what I sought so a towel remained over our window for years. My daughter Mikayla, who was 13, remained at a friend's.

Megan was there at the time of the accident. She was the voice I heard crying and angrily asking if I was OK and trying to draw near.

Chapter 3
AN ACT OF FORGIVENESS

I have tried to recall the accident but the entire day has become a blur. I was told that the children who were at the camp had been gathered in the retreat centre away from the confusion and chaos of the arriving ambulance and the ensuing mayhem. Malachi immediately returned to me after I fell. When friends took him to the barn he paced with anxiety—sweating and frightened very unlike his customary relaxed and calm behaviour. The fall eventually deepened the partnership and connection that Malachi and I had, however, in the weeks following my accident I became increasingly anxious about being near him. I cannot recall how I interacted with him. When I returned to work at the camp I was anxious and fearful and would feel a sense of panic when I would see the children near any of the horses. I avoided the horses and would delegate Jaclyn and Megan to help the children and instruct the riding.

In the following years when I would try to run the summer camps, I decreased the class size, even to just two children but still found the load overwhelming. I was anxious, tired, and continued to experience the

15

dizziness and sensitivity to light and noise, headaches and pain. Before my accident, when we would take the kids on a trail ride I would lead the group with Malachi. I would actually strap a small speaker on his back so I could call out to the kids and we would sing songs as we journeyed through the bush. The children loved the excitement of being away from the restrictions of the corral and off on a grand adventure. After my accident Jaclyn would again choose Malachi as the lead horse, but she said he was different, nervous, and unpredictable.

Malachi continued to express this sense of agitation, which seemed to fade after Doug arranged for a "forgiveness visit" between Malachi and me. I had told Doug that I didn't feel I could go near Malachi again or ever ride again. As they say, if you fall off, get back on again or you will feel fear that becomes paralyzing. Being unconscious was a bit of a barrier to this and so I had not, and would not, ride Malachi again for years. The fear and feelings of guilt and pain would invade our relationship.

One day Doug brought him to the yard below my window and had me peek out to see him. I felt very uneasy, and yet I had a desire to go to him. Doug knew that both horse and rider had been transformed in that single moment of time and a chasm was slowly dividing us to a place where we may never return and he knew this meeting was an important part of the healing journey that both Malachi and I needed to experience.

Walking out to the yard I felt my heart race, my hands shake, my stomach lurch, and my mind filled with thoughts that threatened to end this reunion. Doug however, walked confidently beside me, slowing as we approached Malachi when his head jerked up. I felt my whole body tighten to spring from the danger that I felt when I saw him. Yet he immediately went back to grazing.

I stood back for what seemed an eternity then Doug suggested perhaps I just stand close to him. That first step felt as though my feet were full of lead. It was difficult to move and then I lifted my arm to touch him. The tears flowed and Malachi gently nudged me. I buried my head into his side and allowed the tears of frustration, fear, and pain to flow. Malachi in that moment became the most important healer in my journey to find myself once again. Malachi's name means "Messenger of God" and I believe God had a big wake up call for me in the grand swoon that I had experienced.

Chapter 4

NO TIME FOR REST

The Monday morning after my emergency room visit, I met the kids attending our horseback riding camp with vigor—as I assumed that a weekend of rest was a sufficient amount of time for recovery.

Boy—was I ever wrong. And it was pretty obvious right away.

Within minutes, the chatter from the children overwhelmed me, the conversations with the parents confused me, the questions from the staff frustrated me, the sound of my dog barking each time a car drove up irritated me, and the orchestration of all of these activities exhausted me.

It seemed like my mind had become a trap for noise and light. Even the brilliant sunshine I once adored created a pressure within me that I had never known. My body, brain, and entire being felt tired, and I became paralyzed by feelings of frustration, confusion, and disorientation.

This new reality filled me with a sense of panic and fear as I realized that I could not remain in the presence of the "chaos" of everyday life.

Yet I finished the day and the full week of camp even though I continued to have nausea, dizziness, disorientation, headaches, and pain.

I would often find myself a quiet location away from the chaos and confusion of the camp to help cope with the post-concussion symptoms I was feeling. At noon each day I would go to the house to rest and would remain in my dark quiet bedroom as sleep would provide solace for two or three hours. My dark bedroom and sleep became my only escape from the chaos around me.

Everything seemed to be a haze of activity and I cannot tell you to this day how everything necessary to run a camp, horse farm, and busy family got completed. Yet everything seemed to operate, thanks to my husband, mother-in-law, kids, and friends. I only know that I was exhausted, even sitting watching TV or hearing the pots and pans clang or even utensils hit the plate irritated me and I had to escape to my room time and time again.

Hours and days would pass in a haze that I cannot remember. As I recall this I continue to experience anxiety and guilt that I was neither available, nor helpful to my family during that time. I didn't realize until this year when I was talking to Judy O'Beirn, an acquaintance at a conference who became a fast friend, that I would continue for years to blame and berate myself for allowing this to happen. Yet she noted, it was an accident not something I chose. The weight of the guilt I had carried for years seemed to be lifted in that moment.

I can't tell you how much relief I felt. Having people care for me, complete all of the daily tasks, and keep everything running was so foreign to me. My vague memory of this time with my kids and husband caused me to feel I had let my family down and that I had not been available for my children when needed. Yet in hindsight, I believe I offered my family a more focused, caring, sensitive person than I had been pre-accident. Now that I was unable to balance multiple tasks I would have laser focus on whatever was before me.

When I left the house for my follow-up doctor's appointment during the first week of camp following my accident, I was in a complete haze. As I made my way down the main street of my small town, I felt as though I were walking in slow motion, and even thought—this is what it must feel like to walk on the moon. It was as though I were viewing my experience from outside of my body. The cars and people moved past me in a blur and I experienced them as though I were taking pictures slowly, frame-by-frame. So I looked at the ground as I walked to avoid the visual stimuli that were adding to my headache and making me feel overwhelmed and nauseated.

My doctor said that post-concussion symptoms can be varied and may last for months. There seemed to be no specific interventions to be prescribed and so, being of strong farm stock with a get out there and "git 'er done" work ethic, I would keep moving and pushing myself through the pain, the weariness, the agitation, and frustration as I tried to cope with all of the overstimulation of the camps and the day to day challenges of life.

Each day I would arise believing that I could push my mind, body, and soul beyond the pain, fatigue, imbalance, headaches, and increasing anxiety I felt. The self-inflicted pressures and imagined jeering voices weighed heavily on my mind. "Pull up your bootstraps and get back to it," I told myself along with, "If you aren't busy you aren't worthy," "Oh it will be fine just push yourself a little harder," and "It's all in your head." And of course it was "all in my head". It was a brain injury where unlike a broken arm, the underlying causes were invisible to others. This made it even more difficult to justify my ongoing belief that something truly was wrong with me and that it was not a "simple concussion."

Yet I told myself, if the medical community did not prescribe complete rest and quiet, surely there was no need for me to stay in bed and hide from the rising sense of hopelessness I felt each passing minute.

So I fought the frustration, fear, and anger I was feeling, and got right back to caring for the horses, paying the bills, and doing everything else I had done before. But the exhaustion I felt after even an hour from rising was soul deep and dangerously challenging to my functionality.

Jaclyn Merritt, who had worked for me for the past two years, and my daughter Megan, would continue to run the camp in my absence. I seemed not to be missed as I would often escape the madness and confusion of the camp to the silence and darkness of my room. At the end of the week however, I would remain for the full day for the end of the week show. I believe it was this tenacity and doggedness to remain that exacerbated the post-concussion symptoms. I should have rested and remained in my dark room as I would soon discover.

On the weekend following that first week of camp since my accident I continued to push forward at full-speed, doing payroll, bookkeeping, and a number of other cognitive tasks, until something happened that stopped me in my tracks. The morning of the tenth day after the accident I awoke and found I was unable to speak. Doug had already gone off to work without disturbing me knowing I needed to rest. Alone in my room I picked up the phone to call Jaclyn, who was busy setting up the camp for the day. I accidentally called her mother, a good friend who realized it was me on the other end of the line even though I was only able to make a feeble sound into the phone.

God-incidentally (my saying for coincidence beyond reason), my sister came to my room and whisked me off to emergency. (Mikayla was being dropped off from another weekend at her friend's when I was getting into the car.) Echoes in my mind bounced thoughts back and forth, but I couldn't get my mind to release my thoughts and express them to the doctors or others in the emergency room. I grew frustrated and panicked because I heard people asking me questions, but I couldn't answer. I was given a CAT scan, which revealed nothing "substantial", just minor bruising. This bruising was caused by the bouncing of my brain against the sides of my skull as my head hit the ground at the time of my accident, and without rest, the brain was unable to heal and swelling resulted.

Broca's area is one of the areas of the brain that was affected by my fall. It was the swelling and bruising in this area that had caused my inability to speak. It is in the left posterior portion of the frontal lobe of the left hemisphere of the brain and is associated with language processing. Once again, I was told to rest. But this time, I actually listened to this advice since without my ability to speak—there was not much else I could do. The camps continued with my reliable staff, yet all I could do was lie in my quiet dark room listening to the laughter and joy of the children as they participated in the fun at camp.

It wasn't until several months later that a friend realized I was having difficulty with my speech—problems with word order and stuttering. This was causing me to become more and more frustrated and reluctant to leave the house. I was losing my ability to communicate. My friend referred me to a speech therapist at the community care centre and the therapist began working with me on a weekly schedule. After a few months I began to improve. Then one day she asked, "Did you have an accent prior to your accident?"

I responded "No."

"Well" she said, "You do now!"

I had developed a wee Scottish brogue! Even though I had some Scottish ancestors, I had never been exposed to a Scottish accent other than the occasional television show or movie.

So I made another appointment to see my doctor, and after much testing and discussion, I was diagnosed with "Foreign Accent Syndrome"—a rare medical condition which causes patients to develop foreign accents as a result of strokes, head trauma, or migraines. The doctors said that there was a chance I could one day get my normal speech back, but there was no guarantee. So, I may have this wee

Scottish brogue forever. (And as of the publication of this book, I've still got it.) Would I want to lose it? Well it would be easier shopping without people asking me each time where I am from and then feeling a bit of panic, wondering if I should explain the whole story.

My accent is a funny consequence of the fall and I am only one of approximately 60 people in the world that have been diagnosed with a foreign dialect as a result of stroke or brain injury.

How does this happen? It is truly a mystery. The first accounts date back to 1907 when French neurologist Pierre Marie documented a case in which a Parisian began speaking like a person from Alsace. Karin Humphries, an associate professor at McMaster University who has studied a similar case stated: "Because the cases are so few and far between, it's not quite clear what is happening in the brain to cause the syndrome or what exact part is affected."[2]

So there it was. I had a Scottish brogue and now rolled my r's, shortened my 'ings', and thought everything was "grrraaannd and grrrreeeaat!" I didn't mind the accent, as it seemed normal to me for some reason. Plus, it didn't stop me from doing what I wanted to do nearly as much as my other debilitating post-concussion symptoms. The real challenge was the ongoing symptoms of the concussion that plagued my day and continued to cause anxiety, frustration, and a desire to isolate myself from the exposure to light, sounds, people, and the ongoing nausea, dizziness, headaches, and the difficulty processing the world around me.

My new accent did lead to quite a bit of confusion to my family and friends, who had known me all of my life as a person from Kent Bridge, Canada, not Inverness, Scotland!

---

2   Foreign accent syndrome: Can you suddenly develop a foreign accent? Nicole Mortillaro, Global News: Health, January 8, 2014 3:20 pm http://globalnews.ca/ news/1069235/chatham-woman-who-woke-with-scottish-accent/

Things got even more confusing when I met new people. They would always ask me where I was from. As I debated whether or not to tell the whole story, a look of horror would pass over my children's faces not wanting to endure yet another ten minute account of my situation. Eventually, though, my kid's lightened up since their friends enjoyed coming to our house to talk to the "Scottish mum".

By the way, you may be wondering how I pinpointed the origin of my accent to Inverness, Scotland. In 2010 my daughter Megan was accepted at Herstmonceux Castle in England for her first year of university. Doug and I decided that we would combine seeing where Megan was going to reside for the next year with a trip into Scotland to celebrate our 20th wedding anniversary. As we travelled through Scotland, I called to book a bed and breakfast in Inverness and asked the lady on the phone for directions from our current hotel. She said, "Surely you'll know darlin'. Your accent tells me you're from Inverness!"

This confirmed what I was told throughout our earlier travels in Glasgow, Edinburg, and Oban to name a few—my accent was from northern, Scotland. What a grand surprise and blessing to know where I came from!

Some people would tell me that the accent was more pronounced when I seemed nervous or if I become overtired. During these times, I would laugh and say, "Of course it is. My accent is actually a reincarnated ancestor here to help me out!" It is truly not within my control and at times it can be a bit embarrassing. I recall sitting with my three sisters at a restaurant at Niagara Falls when the waiter asked me where my accent was from. I am sure they thought, "Oh no, not this story." I smiled and told him I had spent time in Scotland and the discomfort of the situation passed and we continued to enjoy our meal together.

Megan and I tried to work at regaining my Canadian accent but it only led to more frustration. I stuttered more with the attempt and found it difficult to find words. As a result, Megan said, "Mom just be who you are. Who cares that you have this accent?" My sister Sandra gave me a plaque with the words "To thine own self be true." written on it and it seemed an appropriate statement in relation to my predicament.

My speech problem may have seemed a novelty, but for me it was a source of serious post-concussion frustration and complications. For example it caused me to miss my nephew's wedding. I had prepared the ceremony, and yet could not perform it because of my stuttering and inability to speak smoothly. I recall my sadness as my daughters prepared to leave on the 300 mile trip from our home to the wedding. My two sisters, aunts and uncles, and friends all made the trek to Halliburton County for the festive event but I remained home.

I recall sitting on the couch crying as they walked out the door, yet within minutes my friend Lana arrived to be with me. Lana seemed to appear when I needed someone to be there. This became an uncanny connection that would occur again and again throughout the next five years. If I was alone and would break down crying or became upset she would just suddenly show up to "see how I was feeling." This was one of the many God-incidences—coincidence beyond normal reason—that would occur throughout my healing journey. These incidents reveal who our true friends really are.

I have two friends, Lana and Becky, who stayed with me, cried and laughed and would just come in the door, head down the hallway and lay with me in the dark quiet bedroom that I was hiding in. When Doug came home he would ask, "So, who has been in your bed today?" I would laugh and tell him which of my friends had visited me that day.

The day of my nephew's wedding Doug had to work again and I sat alone in my dark bedroom watching the time to know when Matt would see his bride walk down the aisle. It was heartbreaking knowing my sisters and all of my family was there and what a great moment it was for my sister Sheila. I have always tried hard to be at the special events for my nephews and nieces and to miss this was excruciating. Just before the moment that the ceremony was to begin I called my friend Beth. She immediately came over and took me to her home because I could barely speak and had broken down crying on the phone. She said it was so unlike me she was scared and immediately came to get me. I would never have been out of control previously nor expressed such sorrow and sadness. I would have just quietly endured it rather than seeking help or the comforting presence of a friend.

Prior to my accident I was able to keep my emotions in check as I would hold sacred space for the families that had lost loved ones during a funeral or beside a hospital bed while someone struggled to cross over. I was sensitive, compassionate, and caring. I was able to support those around me in their loss and comfort them, but after the accident I found this difficult and draining.

The car ride to Beth's was a kaleidoscope of disorientation, dizziness, nausea, and my headache, that seemed to never leave, began to throb. I thank goodness I remained home that weekend and had not attempted to make the five hour drive with my family to the wedding.

I cannot imagine what it would have been like when five minutes was so overwhelming. Within those first few weeks I was robbed of experiencing moments that were so important to me, and yet it was only the beginning of the many disappointments that would arise in that first year, and the years to come.

Diary Excerpt—November 22, 2008

I haven't really been able to write until now. Something has blocked me. Hard to collect my thoughts. I continue to stutter and find it difficult to find the words I need. Ten days after the accident, I lost almost all of my ability to speak. The words were there, but I couldn't get them out. Now, I don't seem to be able to find the words. It is not as bad as it was, however it makes me feel self-conscious and not want to go out. I used to love crowds and meeting new people. Now at times the familiar ones cause me stress and anxiety. I still am unable to drive—something I used to love. I continue to be very tired. Exhausted really by 1:30 pm every day. Physically I must lie down, but mentally I am still racing so I try to rest. The littlest things set me off. I seem unable to make decisions even over the simplest things.

On the positive side—I am at the barn doing some work now, which I love. My back doesn't feel any worse than it did prior to the fall. It really wasn't the fall that hurt—it was my head hitting the ground twice that was the hard part!

I am, I think, spending more time with the girls. I am not thinking of other things in their presence. Not preaching or planning—just being.

It is what I have wanted, prayed, and asked for. Truly it is... while I was preaching in Shetland, I would ask the Lord to let me faint—fall down so others would have to care for me and I could stop working so hard. I was juggling way too many things—not focusing on any one thing. I thought when school was over it would get easier, but it just seemed to get faster.

Be careful what you ask for...it definitely can and will come true—just not exactly as you had planned. I asked to faint—not fall, become unconscious, and have a brain injury.

Chapter 5

WHO AM I?

*O*ur camps continued the following summer. In spite of my loss of voice I could not resist wanting to go down to see the kids and help out. So, in August Doug set up our house trailer at a nearby campsite where I could spend some time away from the noise and chaos around me. This would also stop me from being drawn to the barn where I felt compelled to interact with the kids and help with the chores even though I couldn't cope with all the confusion. Doug somehow knew I needed rest and seclusion which I couldn't get at home. While I stayed in the trailer, he would text me every day to make sure that I was resting, eating, and feeling all right. To this day, he still texts me every day to share a few words of encouragement or to say, "I love you."

After I returned home from the campsite, the days turned into weeks, and the weeks drifted into months. During that time, I flowed in and out of depression, sometimes sinking into the abyss for months. This would lead me to isolate myself even more. The woman I was before the accident had disappeared and I desperately wanted her to come back. The person I was previously became almost like a super hero to me. She acted without hesitation, expressed herself clearly, and radiated humor and fun. She could go for hours doing multiple tasks without tiring. Who was this woman and where had she gone? I began counseling to discover who I had become. I knew I was not able to function as the person I was before my accident, but no one truly knew how trapped I felt inside. Amy Abbruzzese of the Acquired Brain Injury Association of Parkwood Hospital helped me to understand that knowing who I was, remembering all of the tasks and work I could juggle easily and effortlessly previously was actually more of a frustration than help at this time. It was a level I might never reach again.

The work at the barn became the bookends of my day. It gave me purpose and structure. Yet I still had to be directed as to what needed to be done. Usually it was Megan who would go with me to do the end of day chores and she would cue me to what I had to do next. I had established a daily routine of waking and having toast and coffee, showering and dressing and during the day Doug would remind me to rest. It seems ridiculous that this routine would tire me but in the Pacing Points Program from Parkwood Hospital, having breakfast and getting dressed took three of the 15-point allotment for the day. When you added in the chores and helping to make dinner and such, there really was a need to sleep.

But society does not appreciate tiredness and exhaustion. I recall being at an event with Doug when a fellow we did not know leaned over to talk with us and asked what we did for a living. Doug answered confidently that he worked as a grain elevator operator. When it came to inquire of my purpose in life I struggled to find an answer for him. I had been a nurse, fitness club owner, pastor, and an owner and operator of a children's camp but since the accident I only existed. I would like to say that I was operating full time as a mum but I felt incompetent at that as I was unable to help the girls with their homework and extracurricular events. This resulted in less involvement than they had participated in previously. Mikayla had been booking days to go to Toronto to attain jobs for commercials and hoped for modeling or acting. We would have great fun and laughter as we drove to Toronto for the interviews and getting her photos done. After the accident, I barely remembered we had done any of that. I know this was a great disappointment for her.

Our society tends to base your worth on your ability to do multiple things. Previous to my accident I was well respected and appreciated and daresay admired for all I could accomplish in a day. The ability to run multiple businesses and balance work and home was a great coup in the eyes of society. However, it was a false facade as I struggled to keep up with the overwhelming number of tasks. I will now often ask Doug who the heck that person was! I look back now and wonder how I did keep up!

Although I continued to experience the headaches, dizziness, anxiety, heightened sensitivity to noise, lights and crowds, pain from the accident and various other post-concussion symptoms I would have very little professional help. The speech therapist who was the one to recognize my accent and who did a simple cognitive test to help me understand that my processing had been impacted because the executive functioning was affected. I was not "crazy", as I felt and sensed many thought I was. I had experienced a brain injury that had compromised the executive functioning centre that in the past had been so effective.

In the past making a decision was quick and easy. I weighed the pros and cons, spoke with those who might be helpful in making the decision and then it was done. But now I constantly second guess myself. I become anxious if there is a decision between two similar choices or outcomes. I laugh now as my daughter recalls waiting in the grocery store while I was trying to choose between almonds and cashews for a snack. For the life of me I couldn't decide. Honestly I liked both and neither was any better than the other. Megan then helped me immensely by saying "Look mom, if there is a decision to be made and you like both choices equally choose the one given to you first." This would be one of the greatest tools I used and I always chose the first option from then on. For example, at a restaurant, there are so many choices! Potatoes—mashed, baked, or fried? Salad—Caesar or garden. What type of salad dressing? 1000 Islands, Ranch, Balsamic vinegar and the choices would rattle on. Even the waitresses would notice my hesitation and joke about the many choices. I have become more comfortable with this but it really is difficult, especially with so many others waiting for you to make your choices.

My friend Beth did not realize the extent of this indecision until one day she picked me up to go to get a coffee. As we drove in the lane she questioned, "Drive through or should we go in to the café?" She said I looked like a deer caught in headlights as I stumbled to respond. She made the decision for me knowing that I could not handle the chaos of going into the coffee shop.

My favorite coffee, of course, is Canada's #1 choice, Tim Horton's. However, it was many months before I could go in to place my order for coffee as there were always so many in line and everyone seemed to be in a hurry. It was agonizing. I would stand there repeating my order again and again through my mind and waiting in a crowded line where everyone seemed to be so close and wanting to engage in conversation. Previously I would be the one who would initiate the conversation but now, just leave me alone and let me keep repeating in my head my order so I don't go blank when I get up to give my order. Add the stuttering and the inability to process my words and it's easy to understand why I didn't want to leave home—I just wanted to stay in my dark bedroom of solace and solitude.

Before my fall, I was a very active person who could balance five or six tasks at a time effortlessly and most days I would "fly by the seat of my pants." I ran the horseback riding camps with ease. I gave private horseback riding lessons and had school groups visiting the farm regularly. As a pastor of 3 churches, I prepared a Sunday service for 9 a.m., 10:15 a.m., and 11:30 a.m. I also ran confirmation, baptismal and wedding preparation sessions and visited members of my churches in their homes. I was also a mother of two girls, a wife, and a friend. Six months before my fall, I had completed a Masters in Divinity. I always needed to be busy and have a purpose. Before this I was a public health nurse for seven years and then I owned a fitness club for ten years before choosing to go into the ministry. As my husband would joke, "What do you think you will become when you grow up?"

I believe I was caught up in the need to be successful and to always be busy doing something to seem worthy. My ego craved the rush of exhilaration that would flow through me as I rushed from one event to the next, saving and fixing everyone and anything I encountered. Honestly, if I had not fallen I certainly would have burned out. And yet an accident was much more acceptable to society than if I had had a "nervous break-down."

When I was ten years old my mother had a "nervous breakdown". I remember visiting her in the hospital and her crying. We have been told by society that it was unacceptable to be unable to handle the push and rush of society. Why could you not balance and function as a mother, wife, and teacher as well? It was a sign of weakness not to be able to keep up with daily life. My mother was so depressed daily that she would come home after a day of teaching and take to her bed because of the feelings of being overwhelmed by the children all day and the expectations of her position. When I was a teenager I would be angry and critical of her need to seek the solace of her bed. Yet today I would give anything to talk to her about the feelings of stress that she experienced, as I now understand too well how she felt and why she could not go on.

An odd coincidence of the accident is that I began to understand why my mother would have experienced such severe anxiety out in public, and also why my daughter Mikayla would often retreat to her room when others were around. Again, before my accident I was oblivious to this and would always have crowds of people at the barn. If there were not four or five folks there I would pick up the phone and invite others to come. I loved to be surrounded by people yet Mikayla and Doug could not tolerate this. I was sensitive to this however, because by the time the girls got off the bus or Doug returned home I would have everyone gone so it was less disruptive to our family.

A brain injury is not the only reason for higher sensitivity. There are many individuals who, in their day-to-day normal lives, feel the crush and pressure of society and the unease from business and the press of crowds. I believe this was why my mother experienced such high anxiety, depression, and lack of desire to even leave the house. Yet I was unaware of this in my pre-fall personality.

After the accident, I was not the person who wanted crowds or even one or two people around anymore. After we put up the dome I decided that on my birthdays I would hold a concert fundraiser for the special population children who took part in Cindy's programs.

The first year was wonderful! We had Crystal Gage sing and about 120 people filled the dome. It was loud, fun, and exciting. I would attempt to continue this in the year following my accident but found myself overwhelmed, anxious, uncomfortable and stood outside for most of the evening. Although my heart loved the children, I was no longer able to continue these events. It was one more way in which I could berate myself for being unable to contribute due to my accident. In my mind I always fell short of who I was prior to the accident.

Another great disappointment that would add to this was when the special population children would no longer be able to attend our camp. We truly wanted to support and operate these camps but as I tried to cope with the horses, the children, the case-workers who came with the children, and multiple activities being organized I would grow frustrated, anxious, and overwhelmed.

It did not help that this anxiety was increased that summer when Milcah, one of our mares, kicked Kara one of my camp counselors in the leg. Unfortunately my instructions to keep a specific order of horses were not followed by another leader that came with Cindy and panic and chaos ensued. Kara was fine but I was wound up with worry and fear that would not subside for hours.

The proverbial last straw for the camps occurred when a young autistic man grabbed two fistfuls of my hair when I tried to help him off his horse. Two caseworkers could not get him to release my hair and so I stood there precariously praying that Bill, our Fjord workhorse, would not take off! I have three older sisters and they have never pulled my hair that hard! I used my fingernails to encourage him to release my hands but when he did release them he grabbed Bill's ear. This was a recipe for tragedy. I took the lead rope and talked to Bill gently and quietly while the case workers tried to get the young man to release Bill's ear. When he did we quickly grabbed him from Bill's back.

This had been too much! I was exhausted, emotionally and physically tired, and angry with myself for allowing the horse and rider to be put at risk. There really was no way to know that this would occur but I took the full burden of the situation to heart. Previously I would have brushed this off and carried on but after the accident it became too much and we closed the camp.

Chapter 6

LOST

*N*oise and crowds, once familiar and enjoyed, were my enemies, which meant I had to miss several concerts that I was very much looking forward to including Reba McIntyre, Kenny Chesney, and AC DC (Imagine listening to AC DC with a head injury!)

Even three years later when I went to a concert with my husband and friends I thought I would go insane with the press of the crowd, the hum of the voices, the announcements over the loud speakers, the overwhelming smells, and the volume of the concert. I leaned over to Doug within minutes of being seated and said that I had to get out of there. The noise was too much. Either that or I needed ear plugs and upon saying that he went to find them. One of the ushers when asked where he could buy them gave Doug a set as they all wore them while they were seating people. With the assistance of the earplugs, Doug seated on one side of me, and my friend Becky on the other side I was able to watch and enjoy the concert.

Prior to the concert we had gone to Cabelas to do some shopping. Mark, Becky's husband, is an avid duck hunter and so we thought we would walk around and see some of the outdoor gear. Wouldn't you know that when we arrived at Cabelas, they were doing a duck call event! There might have been a few Duck Dynasty calls, but I was not impressed. It didn't take me long to announce that perhaps I would do my shopping from outside the store and window shop!

Before the accident, I was a very strong left-brained individual—it's the left-brain that labels, lists, and thinks logically and linearly. After the accident, I could no longer juggle multiple tasks, make decisions, solve problems, remember details, or organize things. Any sort of disorganization upset me and being asked to make a decision on the fly left me panicked and confused. If someone offered their help, I grew even more frustrated because it only reminded me of what I had forgotten to do or could no longer do. I expressed my frustrations to my husband who suggested to me that there was nothing wrong with being able to focus on only one job at a time, to which I jokingly replied, "I have acquired a "man brain!" (No offence to all the men out there. What a blessing a lot of men have to be able to stay focused on a task and carry it to completion.)

Overall, my life before the fall was multifaceted and sometimes disorganized: My three best friends were Chaos, Mayhem, and Confusion. After the accident, there was no room for these "friends" in my life. My body was exhausted and injured and my mind felt foggy and unclear.

What I really needed was rest. However, I couldn't fall asleep because I feared I might drift off in the darkness of that unconscious veil again. Eventually, my doctor prescribed medication to keep the fears at bay and help me get the rest I needed.

Along with my new physical challenges, I found myself in another struggle. In the midst of my recovery, I was denied long-term disability. The insurance company accused me of "taking too long to recover." This was upsetting and confusing to me. I felt I had provided them with everything they requested to support my claim, yet they continued to deny my long-term disability.

This would become a thorn in my side because not only did the insurance company question my recovery, but others would question my need to stay isolated, remain at home, and be unable to go back to my job in ministry. As I stated earlier, unlike a broken arm, the cause was not obvious and so others questioned the fatigue, sensitivity, and need for quiet. I well understood why individuals who have lost a loved one are angry at the expectancy of society to return to work a few days after the funeral and the agitation as people inquire as to their inability to "move on".

Again it was Judy that helped me to understand that I too was flowing through the stages of grief as Elizabeth Kubler Ross had written about in her 1969 book *On Death and Dying* for those who had experienced a loss of a loved one in their lives. The stages of grief include, in no particular order, denial and isolation, anger, depression, bargaining, and acceptance. These stages are universal but they occur at varying lengths and variable times throughout the process.

I was angry that my cognitive abilities had changed so dramatically and I would through my actions, again and again deny the limitations that I needed to accept. Doug would often come home as I entered into the second year of my accident to find me in the barn throwing buckets because I was so tired and angry. I would have done too many stalls and I could not go on. I would berate myself by saying "Why is someone with a Registered Nursing qualification, a Bachelor of Science in Nursing and a Masters in Divinity cleaning stalls?" I would yell "Surely I am meant for something else!" I would say this not because I felt "better than" doing stalls but I knew God had other plans for me.

Previous to my accident cleaning stalls was a meditation I loved but after the fall I became driven to the task and took little joy in it.

I had truly lost myself. The person I was no longer existed. She literally had died and I needed to adapt to this new individual who seemed to be incompetent, unable to cope, and experienced such severe anxiety that I would nearly vomit as I left the house.

The depression had become so severe that I began to count my meds to see just how many I had and if there were sufficient amounts to just lull myself out of this world. This rash thinking was a result of the cycle of negative experiences and thinking that I could not break out of. I would question in those depressive cycles if my family might have been better off if I had not survived my accident? I felt I was not contributing in a positive way and that I was only costing them more stress and heartache than I was contributing for them.

The financial burdens grew. I had previously been the one to pay bills, calculate and establish the loans for the business, and initiate negotiations for insurance and many of our purchases. After the accident there was an endless stream of paperwork. Bills piled up, due dates came and went, late fees accumulated, payments were declined, and lifelines were severed. I was completely overwhelmed. Yet I didn't reach out to ask for Doug's help. I truly was oblivious to the financial concerns that were arising. Doug believed I was paying the bills and handling things as per usual. However, I wasn't even opening the bills nor was I paying them. Within six months of denials from my long-term disability we received a letter from the bank that our mortgage was in back payments to the extent that they would call the mortgage to be paid.

Sheer panic erupted! When did this happen? I had lost all concept of time. I would later compare this state to Rip Van Winkle. Five years passed and I still believed it was only a day since my accident. To everyone five years had passed and I would always feel that things should remain as they were at the time of my accident. How did I allow this to happen? This was yet another reason to hate who I had become. It was embarrassing, humiliating and led to more anger, fear, anxiety, and depression. We avoided the foreclosure because I was able to borrow the money from my sister Janet to bridge the loan to make the essential payment, but I still could not fathom how we had come to this point!

Yet I had orchestrated the camp's development by mortgaging the improvements and additions such as the dome, the addition of stalls and more horses by leveraging the house and counting on the fact that I would be able to work for the next 7 years full time and also run the camps and lessons to pay the debt that I felt was essential to establish our facility as an all seasons riding facility. Unfortunately, within three months of establishing all of this, I was unable to even manage my own self-care let alone the financial needs of a business that had come to a screaming stop.

Twice in my life now I had discovered that self-employment although empowering and free from the need to answer to a "boss", the freedom of your own choices can leave you in a fragile and tenuous position if your health fails. Although you purchase the insurance for this possibility, I soon discovered that it would not suffice, nor be processed on the timely basis that you were promised.

In the spring of 2010 my lawyer suggested that I have a neuropsychological test done. This is a battery of tests that would conclusively establish if I truly had a deficit in my physical, mental, and psychological abilities. The challenge in attaining this test was twofold. First, the cost was $3500, which the insurance company was not going to cover and so it had to come out of our own pockets, so we cashed in RRSP's to attain one. This began the steady flow of cashing in policies and selling our possessions to finance bills and essentials of day to day life.

Second, most of the neuropsychologists were booking a year to a year and a half ahead. Yet, this was the cornerstone to proving to the insurance company that I had experienced a severe injury. I recall my lawyer telling me that if I felt there was a problem I should go and have the testing done—if I felt it was severe enough. I looked as though there was nothing wrong, yet my speech and processing was self-evident that there was a severe deficit compared to my pre-accident experience.

God-incidentally enough, I was able to get into see Dr. Saudia Ahmad within four weeks. It was a funny sequence of events that led me not only to Dr. Ahmad who diagnosed me with less than 10% ability to process and severely affected executive functioning centre, but also to meet Amy Abbruzzese who would be the first clinician specifically focusing on the brain injury and concussion that I would see.

These serendipitous events began when Mikayla gave me a book at Christmas, *The Tao of Equus*, by Linda Kohanov. Linda's book spoke of work done with horses from the ground rather than in the saddle riding that were having great psychological, social, and physical results for individuals who were finding traditional talk therapy no longer working or needed another way to express and reach within themselves to find the healing presence within. It seemed a bit odd to me in relation to what I had been used to with horses. Although I was a "natural" horsewoman who had done a lot of work through the Parelli Natural Horsemanship program, the goal was always to get on and ride. Yet working with a horse eye to eye to seek answers, insights, and intuitive knowledge was foreign to me. Although I was very interested, I was a bit skeptical due to my scientific nursing education.

I was discussing the book with my friend Becky whose husband I was seeing for chiropractic treatments. She told me that she knew of a man who was doing similar experiential and therapeutic work with horses in Woodsley, which is about an hour from our home. I mentioned this to my husband who became "voluntold" that we were going so I could see what this process was and if I could benefit from it.

Upon arrival, Randy and his assistant Janice, brought two horses into the riding arena and Doug and I were asked to have each of the horses walk over an equestrian jumping rail. The catch was that we could not talk to each other nor could we touch the horses. It became an interesting exercise. Randy would point out later that I stood back and watched Doug take the lead. This was not our pre-fall way of approaching a task. I always seemed to be initiating some new idea for poor Doug to try to integrate and adapt to. Yet these horses were clearly showing us that our previous way of working together had changed dramatically. As we debriefed the situation I began to realize how much Doug had taken on to manage our lives and I was now following his lead. When we got the first horse to go over the rail I stopped to pet him and connect but Doug had already gone to the next horse to begin the task of getting him to step over the rail. We soon came to realize that there was little downtime for him as there was task after task to complete. I had lost the ability to perform many day to day tasks or to motivate myself to complete them.

Another insightful piece that we discovered was that Doug really could think outside the box! The second horse was not as easy to get to go over the rail. He was more interested in the hay at the far end of the arena and chasing his buddy. It seemed forever that we tried to get the horse to go over this rail. I was near the point of exhaustion and frustration when Doug walked over to the side of the building and picked up a whip took the string and placed it around the horses neck and then led him over the rail. Of course I felt we had cheated but Randy explained that this was acceptable. He hadn't told us that we could not use outside items to help us accomplish the task! This was a great insight that encouraged us to look outside of the traditional healing methods to help me overcome the difficulties that were frustrating me.

While we were sitting in the arena Randy discussed his work at the hospital in Windsor with Dr. Saudia Ahmad who was a neuro-psychologist. How God-incidental that I was in need of a doctor with this specialty? Randy said he would let her know of my need for a neuropsychological test and that he would send me her telephone number for me to contact her if she agreed. This was the break with the insurance that I was seeking.

After a few calls Dr. Ahmad contacted me to tell me that she had a cancelation and would I mind coming in on a Saturday? I gladly took the appointment. We talked in her office and reviewed all that had occurred over the two years since my injury. She explained that her assistant would administer the test and we went out to meet her. I recall Dr. Ahmad telling her assistant that I would be determined to do well on all of the tests and that I may experience frustration and anger because the testing was actually set up so that you could not always complete all of the tasks asked of you. For example I would be asked to spell words that were not words that we would have an association with. I do recall becoming very frustrated and angry at one point. It was a full day of testing with just a half hour for lunch with a battery of spelling, math, memory, organization, and fine motor tasks. The events were timed and often I would become frustrated that I was still trying to complete a task when the timer would ring. However, it didn't take me long to complete the mathematics part of the testing as I did the simple adding, subtracting, division, and multiplying easily but when I turned the page to see the fractions I handed the paper to her. She noted that I still had time left to complete the task yet I laughed and replied honestly, "I couldn't complete that if my life depended on it!" So we proceeded to another task.

I had the testing completed in October of 2010, and it resulted in a diagnosis of complete disability as my processing ability was found to be in the bottom ten percent. My ability to process tasks, make decisions, solve problems, and react quickly had been severely compromised. I already knew this, but it was wonderful to have it confirmed that I wasn't imagining things and there truly was a large impairment in my abilities. I submitted the results to my lawyer to issue to the insurance company and waited for the results. It would still be a full year (2011) before it was accepted and the case concluded.

Chapter 7
PUSHING

Yet the book, *The Tao of Equus,* that my daughter gave me continued to lead to interesting God-incidences. After my initial visit with Doug to Randy's facility, I returned to observe an EAGALA (Equine Assisted Growth and Learning Association) training program that he was organizing on his farm. I arrived to discover there were over 20 individuals who were training for their level 1 EAGALA. I was completely overwhelmed by the number of participants and would soon discover that this was a bad decision on my part to even be there and observing.

By lunch I sought a quiet space to eat, as the event was too large for me. As I crossed the yard two ladies asked if I would like to sit with them. I chose to be in the quiet but said I would wander over after I had a bit of time to rest. Upon meeting them one of the ladies told me she had experienced a similar accident and knew what I was feeling. She knew that I had been pushing myself too much to be there and that the people, the noise, the teachings were all too much for me. She referred me to a lady who had been a supervisor at Parkwood Hospital,

44

a recovery and teaching centre for people with acquired brain injuries, and felt I should contact her. She gave me the number and we returned to the event.

By this time I was too overwhelmed, tired, and oversensitive to even sit in the arena. The crowd seemed to press in on me. They began an activity called billiards, which had a team of eight people changing places every 30 seconds to try to get a horse into a "billiards pocket"—a U-shaped area that they were to drive a horse into. I watched as three horses were brought in to participate in this team building game. The play was fast as each player ran to the horses, flapped his arms, yelled to move them, and then the next player in line would repeat the activity to get the horse into a "billiard ball" corner. It became a wild interaction of three horses running, people yelling, flapping their arms and at one point a horse fell to his side. I was so distressed by this I immediately stood up in front of everyone and left the building. My emotions were raw and sensitive and my anger was palpable. I went to the other horses in the barn, took a deep breath and knew that I had to leave. I felt nauseous, my head began to pound, I felt off balance and dizzy. I called Doug and said I would rest in the car before I left to go home and I would take all of the back roads and stop if I needed to.

Trying to participate in events like this, forcing myself to try to perform as if I were not experiencing the dizziness, fatigue, nausea, headaches, spatial challenges, and the ongoing difficulty coping with noise, lights, and crowds always revived memories of who I used to be. Sitting in a crowded arena in the past would not have affected me and I likely would have been someone who would have got up and offered to participate in the events. I would have been upset and moved by the horse falling, but it would not have affected me so dramatically that I would have had to leave in tears, unable to control my emotions.

It truly was the emotional piece that was disturbing to me. I had more intuitive sensitivity but didn't know what to do with it. If people were sad, I couldn't help but cry. If they were angry, I became wound up in it somehow. This flood of feelings made me feel unsteady, like I was a ship on the ocean. (I call it the "wobbles.") I not only felt and experienced extreme emotional volatility within myself, but I also felt it in relation to others who were in the room with me. Have you ever watched *Star Trek: The Next Generation*? Data was an android on the show and he was very logical, practical, analytical, and never expressed or experienced emotions. This was how he was designed to be. In my past I have often idolized this. I would at one point try desperately to meditate daily and strive to hold my emotions at bay. I wanted to keep myself calm and controlled so I would appear in control and be able to help others without burdening them with my feelings or emotions. Like Data I felt I was only to be the key to fixing and helping others rather than needing the help of others or expressing and experiencing their loss or feelings together. I truly felt this was therapeutic for the members of my church.

What balderdash right? Who can be present in the midst of the trauma and loss of a family and not be moved? I would continue to attempt to do this but at the time of my fall this was exacting a huge price from my very soul. So it was with great shock and dis-ease that I realized after my fall that I was an emotional expresser or receptacle that felt, experienced, and expressed all of the emotions of individuals around me. Like Data on the show where he received an emotional chip to allow him to experience emotions, I was crying one minute, laughing the next, angry, frustrated, and then calm and loving soon after. What a roller coaster ride this became.

Later, at another horse event, this time at the Horse Spirit Connections, a centre that was listed in relation to Linda Kohanov's book, I would begin to understand these experiences and begin the process of coping with them.

My farrier Jamie Houghton, who trimmed our horses' hooves, was interested in this event as well and so we traveled together to participate in "Discover Your Inner Self". I was not sure what it really entailed, only that they worked with horses from the ground rather than in the saddle riding, and like EAGALA, it was to be therapeutic, experiential learning with the horse but its acronym was FEEL (Facilitated Equine Experiential Learning).

The group was much smaller, only six participants and the two leaders, Wendy and Andre. The group sat in a circle so it was difficult to choose a chair that was not close to the next person and where my back was against a wall, which is where I am most comfortable when others are in the same room. When my family and I go out to eat in a restaurant they always wait until I have found the chair that has my back to the wall due to my spatial sensitivity. I chose a chair and immediately pushed it back outside of the circle so I was not as close to the other individuals. I had met Wendy previously with my family when we did a detour to their farm while we were at a camping trip. She understood my need to move back and my spatial concerns so she helped me feel comfortable in this choice by explaining a bit as to why I did this to the two individuals to each side of me to ease my embarrassment in having to do so.

The moment I dreaded came when I had to introduce myself. I am unsure if I explained why I had a Scottish brogue and my difficulty processing words together smoothly. I am unsure what I said but I was greatly relieved when this encounter was over and we were able to go to the horses. The first activity was "Meet the Herd". I was unsure what that meant but we were to go to the horses and stand outside of their stalls and without touching them sense what was going on inside of us such as "butterflies in the stomach", tingling, pain, anxiety, and such.

There were ten horses so we were to move around the barn and stand in front of the horses we were drawn to and write down what we felt. I must admit I found this very agitating. I liked the quiet but the aisles felt "tight" even though they were large and spacious and there were only six of us. And of course I felt that I wanted to be doing something not just standing there and feeling what I was experiencing. I felt uneasy, self-conscious, and uncertain.

When the group returned to the centre again we were asked to express what we sensed and felt. Again I felt uneasy, agitated, and uncertain as the individuals around me expressed what they had experienced in great detail. Many were crying as they shared their experience and some had even received a message from the horses. All I could think of was, "You have got to be kidding me? I don't get this!" For someone who for years had tried to squash, suffocate, and dismiss her emotions and feelings to be able to assist others process theirs this only heightened the emotional instability that was raging within me.

I shared briefly that I was a bit uneasy and had felt tension in my neck. Wendy and Andre, who were leading the group were gracious in that they didn't ask me to expand nor focused on my lack of ability to process what truly was happening.

Once again we were asked to go to the horses and this time scan our bodies for sensations and what we were feeling and this led to choosing a horse and then to actually go in with the horses. I stood inside Angelina's stall and felt awkward, inept, and confused. I could hear others crying and expressing deep emotions with their horses. Poor Angelina had lost the lottery when she got me. I stood there barely present and becoming angrier with every passing minute. Yet what I came to discover later is that Angelina was mirroring my presence. She stood off in a corner of the stall, a bit agitated, yet not completely disconnected from me. She would glance over warily at me but knew that I could not draw near nor control the multitude of emotions that were rushing through my mind and body. The 20-minute activity seemed forever.

Once again during the processing of this activity people expressed the beautiful experiences they were feeling in the presence of the horses. It seemed the horses were able to connect deeply and allow them to delve deep within to access wounds that had been there for years. Honestly I could not understand this openness of expression and candidness. I shared briefly and prayed the day would conclude quickly.

Just before the conclusion of the day we were to choose a piece of paper from a basket that had an emotion written on it. The person beside me pulled depression, which was what I felt I could speak to easily, but I pulled exhilaration. For goodness sakes I was feeling anything but exhilarated. This was our homework. We were to reach within our memories of a time we felt this emotion. Again I panicked! How am I to express exhilaration when I felt depressed, uneasy, agitated, and angry most of the time? Yet that evening I was able to reach into the recesses of my mind and retrieve the required memories of times I had experienced exhilaration.

The next day I shared with the group that exhilaration is often interpreted as a "good" emotion. It was often associated with happiness, excitement, resonance, and fun. Yet I confessed that prior to my accident, when I was running between meetings, to teaching, to family tasks I felt the exhilaration of being too busy to even breathe. I was so exhilarated that I could not slow down. I had become addicted to this exhilaration and to the praise I would receive and recognition from neighbours as I was often asked, "How do you keep up with it all?" I was applauded, accepted, and given great accolades because I was doing, doing, doing. I was always busy and moving. This exhilaration actually became like a drug to me. So much so that it led to my exhaustion and prayer to faint, fall, or just have a few days rest in a hospital.

This was the first true sense of awareness I had experienced in years. I now understood why I was trying to work so hard and my addiction to praise, applause, and the "good opinion of others." My soul screamed for rest, release, and solitude yet I smothered it and ignored the signs my body, soul, and mind were giving me.

The second day we participated in two activities. An "energy round pen" and a "reflective round pen." The first activity, the energy round pen, is sensing the layers of connection between yourself and the horse. The layer of connection was evident when the horse would move an ear, swish her tail, or turn to look at you. This would indicate that I had connected with her and I was then instructed to stop my approach and do a rollback (not the Walmart type— just lean back and roll on my heel to indicate an openness and calm) and release a big relaxing "Irish sigh." This was to indicate that I had acknowledged a layer of connection and respectfully waited to feel whether she wanted me to continue to approach or not.

This translates to our relationship with others. Before approaching the horse we were to partner with another person in the group and try to see when we had entered into their "layer of connection." The environmental layer is that which is all around us. This can be a variety of things. It can be the radio, TV, sirens, honking horns, jack hammers and so on. All of these things can be within our environment and we may be conscious of our connection with them or not. Yet whether we are aware of them or not, they can be affecting us.

When I approached my partner, the reaction to my approach was not always obvious. Often the person wasn't aware that they had made a movement, maybe blinked rapidly, or her hands started to move, or lips tightened. But this indicated that there is an awareness of my approach and a need for me to roll back to allow that person the space and time to adjust to my approach.

What a concept, right? Actually being respectful, sensitive, and allowing that individual to have just a moment to adjust and breathe prior to my approaching further. You have likely felt someone nearing you and you connect to the thought of her approaching but your body has already made the connection. Your body tensed a bit, your breathing shortened, maybe your jaw tightened.

I was at a funeral recently and I could tell from across the room that when this fellow went to stand up he was going to come and talk to me. How did I know this? Before my brain connected, my heart sensed this movement first. All of us have this heart sense, but some are more sensitive than others and since our environments are usually crowded, noisy, and rushed, we lose this subtle knowledge of the layer of connection.

It is something inside of you that speaks to you, heightens your awareness, and tries to connect with you so you are more aware of what is happening around you but often ignored. This is our "intuitive mind" and it is as important as our conscious thoughts. The Institute of HeartMath has revealed that the heart is stimulated at the same time as the brain. The heart has neurons similar to the brain and scientists have proven that the heart sends intuitive signals to help us be more aware and manage our lives.

Intuitive Awareness

By bringing our attention to our heart and holding positive emotions of joy, compassion, and appreciation it is possible to induce intuitive feeling and physiological understanding.

How do we do this?

While doing a breath meditation, breathe slowly and deeply for three to five minutes.

Then think of a positive feeling or of an experience in which you have felt happy, relaxed, and filled with joy.

Hold this feeling and continue the meditative breath for at least five minutes.

This will synchronize the harmony between your heart, brain, and body helping you to feel calm, centered, and a sense of ease.

To enhance this do the breathing of joy filled memories with your hand over your heart, which will connect you even deeper to this awareness.

Do this exercise three times per day for three to five minutes and you will begin to connect deeply within and sense intuitive expressions from within.

The more you do this the more connection between the heart and brain will develop and you can access your feelings of intuition and emotions deeper and deeper to create harmony within.

In the energy round pen we were given the opportunity to connect to this intuitive "heart felt" awareness and develop the physiological understanding of the synchronicity between the heart and brain. We were able to delve deeper into the relationship of heart, mind, and soul by connecting to the awareness within during our interaction with the horses.

As we sensed the layers of connection with the horses in the round pen, we were asked what it felt like within our bodies. I soon discovered that my hands were tingling and pulsating to this connection with the horse and my "gut" would tighten.

This heightened awareness also translated into setting a boundary with the horse experience in the round pen. If the horse was approaching me and I felt I did not want him to advance any closer I used the "wand" (a stick) to mark a line in the sand. You have got to be kidding me right? A 1,500 pound horse is coming towards me and all I have to do is mark a line in the sand and he will stop? It seemed impossible but it actually works.

Linda Kohanov in her book *The Tao of Equus* had an epiphany of awareness with her horse Midnight Merlin. He was a big black stallion that had to be kept in an isolated corral because his previous training had made him dangerous and unpredictable to handle. He was big, gregarious, and strong. Linda however became aware that these outbursts of anger were followed by confusion, vulnerability, and shame. She realized he had many symptoms that veterans with PTSD felt. From this awareness she was able to teach the stallion how to integrate into a herd, yet this also assisted her to tap into what she calls a "fierce sensitivity" in herself. She began to teach Merlin strong but compassionate acceptable boundaries to help him learn to socialize with others and release him from the confines of separation and isolation.

This translated into my experience as I had always loved to be around people. I loved to get to know people and share with them, but since the accident I had begun to resent being with people. I did not want to make small talk while waiting in the lines anymore. Just leave me alone. I would become agitated, angry, and frustrated and would divert my eyes down so I did not make eye contact that might encourage others to start a conversation. This would lead me to feel isolated, and like Merlin, ashamed and confused by my reaction to others.

It was in setting boundaries with the horses, drawing the line in the sand to stop the horse's approach, respecting my own need for space and breath that I was able to re-engage with strangers again. I believe that I had developed an "intuitive sensitivity" after my accident, which was strange and overwhelming for me but I know many others have had this "gift" all of their lives. I was just not aware enough to recognize the difference. I am sure that I had been an "innocent agitation"—

unknowingly overwhelmed others—by my enthusiastic and caring desire to connect with people anywhere in line at the bank, Tim Horton's, even when drying my hands in the washroom! It wasn't wrong, but now I feel a more quiet concern and caring rather than just the unrestrained desire to connect.

This too is mirrored in the horse interaction in the energy round pen. Once I have set the boundary, I can either hold that by standing straight, my body strong in thought, mind and spirit indicating that the horse was not to approach further, or I could relax, roll back and do my Irish sigh to allow the horse to continue advancing towards me. Often when I am teaching others about this I will refer to setting a curfew for teens. If I say that my daughter should be home at 1 a.m. and she arrives at 2 a.m., I need to set the boundary and be clear that this was unacceptable. If not it will be 3 a.m. the next time.

Setting clear boundaries in a relationship can be difficult. We feel we are offending others if we state that we need a quiet moment rather than being open to a conversation or exchange when someone begins one. After my accident my daughter Megan would spontaneously come up and hug me and I would tense and step back to avoid it, which I am sure, was confusing for her. Yet I would feel an overwhelming sense of panic as she embraced me, and then a rising sense of shame and regret that I couldn't return the hug spontaneously. After all, she was only expressing her love.

The activity with the horses translated to this experience with Megan as I learned to become more aware of my personal space, sense her approach, and say, "Wait—you have to ask me if it is ok to hug me." We joke about it now, and she will hug me just to get a wee rise out of me, but that is because I have honed the skill of sensing her approach, checking in with my own feelings and comfort level, and am able to tolerate the restricting embrace. Interesting right? All of this is just below the level of our conscious awareness and it took a horse to teach me this! And it is in this conscious awareness that I can initiate change in my life.

Conscious Awareness

When we connect to conscious *awareness* we can decide what we think, say, and do.

We can focus our *attention* on what we desire regardless of the current situation we see ourselves in.

We can *imagine* what it is like to already have, sense, and feel what we desire.

We form a mental picture of what this will look like and connect it to emotions of joy, happiness, and love (as we did in the breathing exercise above) and connect that to which we desire to feel in our current and new state of being.

A change of the circumstances around you can change through the conscious awareness and focused attention to this new desired state. This is what the horses assist us to do in the round pen. They help us gain awareness in their mirroring of our current state of being, and we can maintain our state of being, by a conscious decision to do so. As we improve our intuitive sense in relationship with them we can see where we are and as such decide where we want to go.

My experience with the horse Angelina turned the tables on me. I respectfully approached sensing the initial layer of connection and then would continue my exchange until I came to a point where I knew if I approached any closer I would be invading her personal space, which was indicated by her ears laid back expressing a clear "Whoa there—this is where I feel comfortable with you—please stop." I so wanted to touch her though. I wanted to go up and stroke her to let her know I was friendly, compassionate, and wanting to connect. Yet I had to respect her indication that she was not comfortable with me approaching any closer. The setting of boundaries is a delicate balance involving establishing desirable limits, justifying them, making them understood, and not offending those involved. These principles apply to horses, people, and to many other creatures as well.

When we are weak or "wishy, washy" in setting a boundary, the other person (or horse) may have no idea what we really want. We correct them when they cross one boundary, yet the next time they cross it we don't, which could be confusing to anyone. Once you set a boundary you must state it clearly to ensure they understand then stick by it. You will not offend someone by setting a clearly defined boundary or expectation in your life. It is when you aren't consistent that others will become offended or hurt due to a misunderstanding.

So I stood respectfully about an arm's reach away and waited until things became comfortable for both of us. Remarkably when I concluded the activity by walking to the gate of the round pen to get out, she followed me. Even though I had not touched her, our connection was authentic and deep. It was in this respectful exchange that we connected more deeply than I ever could have by just walking up, without any awareness of her level of comfort, and petting her, or throwing a halter on her.

It was this patient abiding that deepened our connection to a level of trust that enabled her to follow me, which was achieved by just standing quietly in her presence. Prior to my accident, I would be in the presence of others frequently but never be present. My mind would be flying to the next activity. I would be writing a sermon in my head, or calculating the budget for our business. I thought others didn't realize this but I know my daughter Mikayla knew when I wasn't fully present for her.

Mikayla has sensitivity and insight into others that I lacked completely pre-fall. I know visitors to our home would feel she was perhaps being rude, as she would rarely come out of her room to join us. Yet at some point, she would walk by, politely stop and make an exchange of niceties, and then go back to her room. Now, I have to admit at 15 or 16 years of age, this is a typical teenage behavior, but I gradually became aware that it was deeper than that. It was a discomfort with being in the presence of others. This vulnerability that she had experienced throughout her younger school years would find me explaining to teachers that she just needed time to get the concepts.

Mikayla would experience such anxiety that concepts she would learn one day could not be remembered the next day. This led to frustration, embarrassment, anger, and an inner struggle and confusion that none of us around her recognized. I couldn't understand why she hated to go into a store alone to make a purchase, but I do now. As I enter the store the walls seem to close in, conversations and the background music blare in my ears, and the look of the helpful employees makes me walk faster and divert my eyes. I can feel my heart pounding and can hardly breathe until I can make my purchase and get out of there. My head injury has heightened this sensitivity for me, but I now know that there are many others who experience this and I was just not aware of it. So to those I irritated with my overly friendly demeanor pre-fall—I apologize.

Chapter 8

EGO—EDGING GOD OUT

*I*n the afternoon we were to do a reflective round pen. We were asked to pick a horse, which was taken to the round pen inside the arena. I then stood outside the round pen, and Andre, one of the instructors, led me in a body scan. This scan was to help me truly feel what my body was experiencing. I was to connect to each area and determine if it was in pain, too cold, too hot, if I felt tingles, perhaps even a colour or any other feelings or thoughts that might arise during the scan. If a particular area came to my attention I was to breathe into it and sense if there was a message from that particular part of my body.

Really? You can imagine by this point that I am feeling uncomfortable and self-conscious. The "false self" began rearing its ugly head again to block me from truly focusing on what I needed in that moment. Self-deprecating thoughts raced through my mind. "What are the others thinking?" "Am I doing this right?" "I can't think." "Man, I feel stupid." "Why can't I relax like everyone else?" Which was the problem—I wasn't supposed to be thinking I was to be sensing and feeling. I was allowing what Andre called the "itty bitty shitty committee" to run wild through my mind.

This is the ego's way of keeping old paradigms within us. As I stated earlier, my ego during the horse activities was in full gear. The ego is essential to our well-being but when it over reacts and blocks our ability to proceed, or causes us to be disingenuous in our relationships it can be very harmful. It was my ego that engaged on the day of my accident. When Malachi took off and unseated me I was embarrassed because there was a group of grandparents, parents, friends, and siblings that had come to watch the end of the week show for the kids. My response to Malachi's fear was one driven by ego, not by compassion and concern. I played to the crowd to create humour and cover the embarrassment and increasing fear I was feeling.

If I had just put my hand down and rubbed Malachi's neck and said "eeeeaaassssyyyy—there's a good man", as I do on the trails when his fear level may be rising, I know I would not have fallen off. Here are some additional beliefs that ego may hold that we are not even aware that we have.

It was ego that bid me to play to the crowd prior to my fall rather than calming and comforting Malachi through his fear. For if I had chosen compassion rather than reaction I would have never fallen.

The ego can influence us in positive and negative ways. The ego is essential to our well-being but if the ego has adopted paradigms that ignite scarcity, criticism of ourselves and others, thoughts of unworthiness, dis-ease as a norm, fear, lack, and adversity then the ego can be a strong opponent in the quest for abundance, vitality, harmony, success, and authenticity.

The ego holds five beliefs

First the ego may believe that what I have is a measure of my worth. It is this state of ego that initiated the phrase—"The one who dies with the most toys wins!" We evaluate ourselves not only by what we have but also in relation to what we have compared to others. Am I keeping up to the Jones'? And if I can't—then I am failing.

Of course this is not true. You are a divine child of God produced with a purpose and with such uniqueness that there is no one else in the world like you. And so it is not what you obtain, gain, acquire, and hold that determines your value.

As a matter of fact this is a game that you will lose as it is almost impossible to keep up with technology, new toys, and gadgets. And I rarely see these pieces sitting in anyone's coffin when they die.

Second the ego tells us our worth is based on what we do for a living. You may have adopted the belief that if you are working at a job that you get down and dirty to do that it isn't as valuable as a person sitting at a desk pushing paper or making six figures. Let's clear that up shall we? There are people who are skilled at paperwork, sales, swinging the big deals, but they wouldn't be there if there weren't people cleaning her office, scrubbing the toilet, taking out the garbage, waiting on her for lunch, and fueling up her car. These are not less worthy jobs. They are essential! Have you ever been in a city where the garbage collectors went on strike? Hello! They are very essential!

You have gifts and talents that are unique to you. Perhaps you can't design a bridge, or balance a budget—but you have special gifts that are unique to you. You just need to take the time to acknowledge them, give thanks for them, and know that your true worth is the belief in yourself that you are unique, worthy, and a divine creation.

Third—The erroneous belief that I am my reputation. I love the title of the book *Your Opinion of Me is None of My Business*. I wish it were a universal pledge that—as my mother often wisely reminded me "If you can't say something nice do not say anything at all!" Have you ever been in a room with people who love to bring up dirt about others? Do you ever think when you leave "I wonder what they are saying about me now?" Loyalty means loyalty in presence and absence. No one is perfect. We are all human. But making your decisions based on the "good opinion of others" is a burden that is unworthy of you! Remember you are a divine being, created in the image of God and worthy of love, abundance, well-being, and success! Let me repeat that you are a divine being created in the image of God worthy of love, abundance, well-being, and success!

The first three beliefs that your ego may hold, to get more stuff, do more, and to get folks to like you, are powerful motivating factors that in many cases will lead only to exhaustion, paranoia, and stress. How do we overcome these limiting beliefs? We overcome these by frequently using an affirmation of forgiveness and acceptance.

Write, read, repeat this over and over again. "I release and forgive myself for any beliefs that are unworthy of God, of my true worth in my mind. I am whole, powerful, strong, loving, worthy, deserving, and a perfect creation of God. I am loving and I am loved and I am thankful for this day."

These are not ego driven self-centred statements. They are true. You wouldn't be here if you were not an expression of love and I am not talking about personal love of parents, family, and friends, but of a greater universal love. A love that is so powerful that if we all felt this presence and worth within ourselves and each other, I believe we could overcome wars, poverty, and dis-ease that our world is experiencing. Truly if you feel you are a worthy expression of divine love you cannot but be kind to yourself and others, which I feel is the true reflection and purpose of our presence on this earth.

This leads us to the fourth false belief of the ego. It is the belief that I am separate from everybody else instead of connected through the universal source that we all emanate from. We are one. As I often say to my children, we are all different but we are also the same. And if we originate from the same universal source, then if I hurt you, I am hurting myself. Let's put it this way, we are all from the same cookie dough, and it was in the separation of source, or of the cookie dough into separate cookies, (I know this is simplistic but it is this simple) our division into each individual that gave us the illusion that we are separate beings. But we are not. We are unique and that is the gift of the separation. Yet the true source of all being is as one. The Universal One is and always has been the substance of all being. The simplest message of all is in the Disney movie *The Lion King, We Are One.*

This leads to the fifth false belief of the ego, which is that we are separate from God, separate from our universal source. The Universal One, the Presence, Breath, Chi, Essence of Life is not outside of you but dwells deep within you. And when you feel separated from the universal source, you feel lonely, disconnected, and dissatisfied. I truly believe that our sense of separation from God, our universal source, chi, whatever we shall call it, is our greatest reason for discontentment. It is what I feel is our truest and deepest longing, a connection to our source. Augustine stated it well—"God is closer to me than I am to myself." Yet paradoxically he wrote "restless is our heart until it rests in you, O God".

It is true the first part acknowledges our deepest longing and the second part recognizes that we will remain restless until we truly find that the ultimate meaning is in the intimate connection to our source. What we feel we are missing from life is already within us. To create harmony within we must go within to connect to our most creative, loving expression of ourselves to reflect upon the world.

The ego can lead us to repeating patterns, habits, or ways of thinking that we have adapted or adopted from the individuals, environment, and circumstances that surround us. Dr Wayne Dyer calls these 'memetics'—which are behaviours that are repeated and passed onto others. It is the transferring of ideas, attitudes, or beliefs to others, which is done mentally—it is in your mind and this will influence your behaviour. The mind is mimicking and imitating what it sees and hears and embeds it so deeply within your subconscious they become automatic responses and repeating behaviours.

They are what we have heard throughout our lives that have implanted themselves into our subconscious. It may be cultural conditioning that has made us believe that we "are not good enough", "are not smart enough", "you are poor", or perhaps "you are lazy" and this illusionary thinking has now become your own. It can actually be passed from generation to generation, from mind to mind, but it is not truly who you are. It was that which you have absorbed into your subconscious right out of your crib.

But once these beliefs are programmed into your unconscious it starts to influence your behavior in very subtle ways. You act in certain ways to accommodate your label, your designation that others have assigned to you.

As I stood in the round pen, it was this conditioning that made my mind race while I was doing my body scan and setting my intentions prior to going into the round pen. It was the ego that was to minimize what was really happening for me. I mentioned this to the leader who then asked what my arousal level was. Oh for goodness sakes! I was anxious but not because of the horse. I was anxious and my arousal level had gone up because I was feeling so self-conscious. Yet Andre pressed for me to identify the number between zero being I am almost asleep to ten feeling like I was going to run wildly out of the building. I was at a six.

I was then told to turn to the horse and state if that number had increased or decreased. I must admit for a brief moment my heart raced as I looked at the horse. She was standing right at the gate when I turned but within moments my anxiety level decreased. I said it had now returned to 6.

Andre then instructed me to connect our hearts imaging invisible fibres running from my heart to the horse's heart. With this sacred attachment I was to state my heart's desire to attain in the interaction with her. To be honest I can't remember what I desired. Again my ego took over and I could not think nor connect to my body to ascertain what I truly wanted. I believe I mumbled something about "learning from the horse".

Yet I can remember the young girl who sat beside me, and what she desired to attain in her heart connection with Thor, the large black Percheron she had chosen. She had stated that she wanted to rid herself of the "previous 100 years of past traditions." As I watched this young girl enter the round pen and engage with the large black horse I became mesmerized and engaged in their interaction that consisted of standing and looking at each other from a distance of about two feet. The young woman would shed tears quietly as they stood gazing at each other. Somehow while they were locked in this silent depth of interaction, I too became part of this sacred interchange of communication that was much deeper than words or actions could convey. As I watched their exchange I began to weep. And I do not mean silent tears of compassion. I was sobbing uncontrollably. I buried my head and tried to hide the depth of my emotion but it was obvious to all outside of the round pen that I was experiencing emotion much deeper than I had ever thought possible.

This exchange seemed to open a glimpse of possibility for me. I saw how the honoring of authenticity could open to honest emotion and release the pockets of darkness that had invaded my life. It was in that moment that I began to understand what the others were experiencing, conveying, and exchanging with the horses throughout the last two days. The horses were mirroring their honesty, openness, and desire for relationship and expression.

This was something I wanted to express to Doug upon my return but could not. It was an experience beyond words and I found it difficult to share. I could barely process the experience and emotions I felt and so it seemed impossible to share this depth with those outside of that experience. Yet I had changed. It was ever so slight, hardly noticeable, and certainly nothing I could express, but I felt a shift deep within that seemed to sense possibility.

Chapter 9

A New Approach

Upon my return to our farm I approached our horses with a renewed respect and authenticity. I no longer just approached and forced myself into their space but would approach with respect, invitation, and heightened awareness. This was most noticeable with our black horse Midnight. Previous to this workshop I would go out to the paddock, walk to Midnight who would usually begin our interaction with nips and pushes that would result in me angrily demanding respect. Yet with this new awareness I stopped a few feet away when he turned an ear to me recognizing that I had entered his layer of connection. I engaged awareness, breath, and paused to allow him that moment of connection and then something amazing happened. Rather than nipping and nudging me, it was him that approached me with confidence and an eagerness to see why I was there. Yet when my phone rang a few minutes later into our exchange he returned to his prior self-expressing insecurity and fighting for attention and dominance by nipping and pushing again.

It was through this exchange that I began to understand the art of communication and how much we are saying without words in our everyday exchanges. I was saying to Midnight through my actions that the phone call was more important than the connection we were sharing. Soon he was nipping and pushing me again to the point that I had to crawl between the rails of the fence to get out of there because he was starting to play rougher. I had placed myself in danger by answering the call in the midst of the horses because when you are not truly present with them physically, spiritually, and mentally, they can accidently hurt you by one horse shoving into another. They were teaching me that being in the moment, staying present to those around you is the true present that we receive in our interaction with others.

Your body language presents reams of information to those around you and if you think your thoughts are only heard by you—you are wrong. Many of the critical condemning and comparing thoughts we think in the presence of others is actualized in our relationships. As Neville Goddard wrote in *The Power of Awareness*—"Others only echo that which we whisper to them in secret."[3] So be careful what you think or image in your mind in relation to others. It will surely be as you say and imagine it to be.

I know this to be true from an activity I was doing with Malachi that reflected my thoughts rather than my intention. My intention was to take a "carrot stick", which is a Parelli training stick with a "savvy string" on the end and flip the string around with more and more movement but without him moving. This is communicated to him not only by the movement of the stick but also through my nonverbal body language, my energy level in the movement and also my thoughts. I repeated this activity for a very long time over months but Malachi would continue to move even though I tried to relax and to communicate ease rather than movement.

---

3   Goddard, Neville *The Power of Awareness*, Pacific Publishing Studio, USA

I finally discovered that in my mind I was telling Malachi to move. A Parelli instructor had come to do my Level 1 certification in which it was necessary to play this "friendly game." It was not until the instructor told me to think of being on vacation, go somewhere you love and see clearly what is there and how you feel. It was then that Malachi remained still. Previously I didn't believe that he would stand still. I continued to say over and over again in my mind "He is going to move" "He doesn't trust me" and so of course, this was reflected back to me.

Once I became aware of this I was able to think congruently with what I desired. It was in his mirroring to me what I was thinking beyond my conscious awareness that I truly was able to focus renewed attention.

The retreat weekend and the new way to interact with the horses began my journey to healing. I attribute my true ability to heal from the inside out to the horses in their quiet honoring presence and insightful reflection as they mirrored my journey of loss of self and the birth of a new person.

July 28, 2009

I took the camp sign down yesterday. I have my harmony back! I return to Creating Harmony Spirit Centre.

Selah

It is funny the way I progressed in relation to naming what my accident was. I began by calling it "the great fall", as it seemed to be like the journey of Adam and Eve, I was kicked out of the garden of paradise of my previous life. Over time I began to call it "the wee fall", as the fall began to lose its significance as I saw it contained blessings and possibilities for insights that I would never have known if I had not fallen. Now I just call it "the horseback riding accident". The fall began to be less significant as the horses were leading me to epiphanies of a deeper knowledge of myself, of my family, and the lessons I am learning.

My most valuable lessons have come straight "from the horse's mouth" or at least from my interactions with them over the last five years. I am sure my neighbours and those around us have often wondered why we have not sold or given our horses away. It is because they have healed me, welcomed me into a community of quiet, honest, authentic, presence in which I have never been compared to another, criticized for feeling a certain way, condemned for my choices, or gossiped about.

At a crucial and stressful time of financial decision Doug suggested that our three original horses, Ice, Midnight and Melchizedek should be sold so we could save on expenses. This is the one, and I believe only time, that I threw the f-bomb at my husband. Prior to my accident I had mentioned selling them on a number of occasions and had been met with total disagreement from Doug. He said that he would rather sell our tractor before we had to part with one of our beloved horses. And now it was my turn to offer to sell anything rather than selling the horses as I became aware of just how much they had contributed to my healing.

They truly had become my community. This became more and more a reality as I began to isolate myself from others and from leaving the property unless forced to.

Chapter 10

OVERCOMING OBSTACLES

I returned to Wendy and Andre's to participate in their "Horse Medicine" workshop in December of 2009. This was focused on spiritual growth through the wisdom of a horse. It interested me because of the spiritual component and Wendy felt it would be healing for me mentally, physically, and spiritually. This time my daughter Megan drove me and stayed at the farm while I participated in the three day workshop.

Again I felt overwhelmed when people started to arrive. The noise of conversations before registration, chairs sliding, the door opening and shutting, the clang of coffee cups, and the overall noise irritated and created so much anxiety that I wanted to bolt. There were two things I would do when overwhelmed by noise and crowds. One was to leave and find a dark, quiet spot to get away from the confusion. At home I would retreat to my bedroom, but here it seemed impossible to get away from it, so I choose my second strategy, which was to sit in a semi-conscious state praying for the noise to stop.

Once again we had to share who we were, where we had come from that day, and I know I pressed through it saying as little as I could just to get the attention away from myself. We were asked to visit the herd, and to write down in our journal words, thoughts, colours, sensations etc. that we feel as we walk about the stalls. I felt more at ease with this and actually wrote words this time.

Dusty: without expectation
Angelina: welcome, heal
Thor: allow, be yourself
Aria: stretch, let it out, BE
Paris: Be thou my vision

I had developed a connection to the horses, an ability to be present, to listen, to allow, and to trust—yet I still felt exposed and vulnerable.

Later that morning Andre led us on a drumming journey. As instructed I felt myself encased in a raindrop that burst open in joy to land in a grassy area where my horses dwelt. I looked around this place that Andre said to imagine as safe and glorious. A place where I could return at any time to find the peace, calm, security, and the solitude I desired. To the east I saw a stag at the edge of a forest, to the west an Indian chief standing by a fire upon a precipice, to the south a lake, and to the north another large forested area. It was safe, quiet, and peaceful.

Andre continued a steady beat on the drum as I looked around this place of peace and he invited us to become a horse; to embody the experience of being this majestic divine creature. In that moment I forgot all that was around me and truly sensed and felt the muscles, the sinew, the strong beat of my heart like that of a horse, the feeling of four feet upon the ground, grounded and strong. I felt the sheer power and strength, the joy, to run to the herd and play, kicking, and rearing, twisting and nipping playfully. What a sense of power, freedom, and grace!

When Andre led us back slowly through the journey to return to reality I did not want to release the joy and strength I had experienced in being the horse. It was exhilarating and powerful as I had not felt that way since my accident and I wanted to stay immersed in this experience. Yet slowly I returned to the present and to the group. Andre did not want us to lose the feelings and sensations of being the horse and so we were not to talk to anyone around us but to go straight to the horses. I had chosen Thor earlier to participate with in this exercise, and in the silence like in a dream I headed to see him. What fun it was to stand in this giant horse's stall and still sense the strength and majesty of the horse I had embodied. He actually nipped me, which worried Wendy, but to me it was what a horse would do to another horse and so I was not offended or harmed.

Unlike humans, horses do not take offense to a clear setting of a boundary. The bite would have been somewhat like a short retort from a person to correct something you might have said or done. Yet the horse would not walk around for the rest of the day ruminating over this small offense and discussing it with the other horses. As humans, many of us seem unable to let small things go. We seem obsessed with the drama that can arise from a small offense to rumor and share it in hopes that others would concur with us that we had not deserved to be treated in this manner rather than going to the individual that presented this slight offense, clearing it up, then letting it drop. It is one of the greatest reasons why I wanted to stay in my dark room.

Yet in the presence of Thor at the Horse Medicine workshop I could just be me. Under the influence of his quiet confidence and strength I adopted these same feelings and emotions. I felt stronger, clearer, and more confident. It was wonderful to be in his presence and know that

I would not be judged. He would not speak of it to anyone; he would not begin an uncomfortable conversation about himself or others, or condemn me for the time it was taking to heal. He did not doubt that my symptoms were real or believe my stuttering speech and accent were crutches I was making up to not return to work. Perhaps you can see that I had developed a fear of interaction with others and had become more and more of a recluse.

Were people really saying these things? It may have all been imagined but it seemed very real to me. The counseling I was receiving from my social worker Jane was helping but I was starting to use the prescribed medication to induce sleep so I was unable to leave my room, or I would turn to alcohol to smother my feelings and feel more at ease and released from the body that entrapped me when I was out with others. I have had a few incidents that I can say were embarrassing, out of character, and revealed how truly desperate, angry, sad, and depressed I had become.

In the afternoon of the third day at the Horse Medicine workshop we did a journey ride. My journey ride was with Brasita. I would sit on her while she was being led, with a guide on each side and then I was blindfolded to trust in the horse and this journey. At first I was nauseous, dizzy, and disoriented and that was when I was just standing beside her! Yet I knew I had to do this. It was a journey I needed and wanted to take, so I stepped up into the saddle and heard "Let go; release." It began to rain and the elements enhanced my fears and the roaring within my mind and thoughts. I knew I had to let go of the incessant nattering within my head and draw from within to truly experience this ride.

Wendy repeated again and again "Breathe Sharon. Just breathe." She asked me "What is it you need to release?" First was the expectation of who I thought others wanted me to be. Second was fear. Relax and be. Just be. Third, was judgment that I sensed from others. Let them go she encouraged; release and let go. I felt as though I would vomit. I literally leaned forward and felt my stomach heave. I was shaking and Wendy asked me "What do you need Sharon?" I needed to trust and let go. I needed to believe. I was told by my Spirit guide to "play, enjoy, to be, to relax and not worry so much."

I was then told to use my voice. At first I barely let out a sound and then it began low within my vocal chords and then it resonated within my chest and I sang "hey—oooooo". The note seemed to hang forever within my chest and I threw my head back. I felt free! Let it flow!

I was told to look in a mirror. Who was looking back at me? I saw an older woman with her hair tied up and the rest flowing in the breeze. She was serene and beautiful, happy, vibrant and peaceful. She gave me a gift of a crystal, which I am to carry to remind me of the woman "I Am"—one of confidence, peace, strength, wisdom, and hope to others so they know of the divinity within.

The God-incidental part of this was that the woman I "saw in the mirror" was one that would be described to me—her look, poise, confidence, and strength—by five different people who catch a glimpse of truly who I Am. One would see this image of me as I crossed our yard to speak with her, another while walking the labyrinth with her, another while I was exiting a round pen experience with Contender, yet another across the room at a conference, and lastly while I was having breakfast in a restaurant, the lady across from me began to tell me of who she really saw sitting across from her. I believe they see the previous person I was in the Scottish highlands centuries ago that somehow I now have resurrected within me after the accident.

I will pause here before continuing on the retelling of my Horse Journey to answer the next question I know you are experiencing. "Do I believe this is a past life experience I have tapped into?" I must admit that having these five individuals, who do not know each other and in different times and places describe to me that as I walked to them they saw me as a woman with her hair half braided at the top and the rest falling around her shoulders of reddish blond hair. Each time

I am described as tall and slender with a bow and quiver. And each description characterizes her as regal, poised, exuding strength, calm presence, and regency.

I have, through a workshop with Brian Weiss, done a past life regression exercise. He led us through an exercise that placed us in the womb to be born. The exercise was about an hour in length and I had a moving sensate memory of being born to a Celtic tribe in the hills. I was the daughter of a Druid and a High Priestess. I recall being eight years old and riding in front of my father on his horse to go out to see his people. At one particular fire was a man, Liam 18 years old who teased me and bowed in feigned honor "Good eve High Priestess". This man resonated with me, made my cheeks blush even at this young age, and I kick him in the shins.

As I grew I was honored and respected for my skill with the bow and warring, although I do not feel the High Priestess was to be the warring member. Nevertheless, I saw myself out on the battlefield and a vision of Liam who is now 28 with me leading our clan. I am then struck down with an arrow in my left shoulder and Liam carries me to a safe place. I see Liam leaning over me looking into my eyes. We have always had an attraction that was forbidden, yet in this moment I know in his expression the deep love we have for each other. At that point Brian says, look up and see who is in front of you. To my shock, it was Doug's face that I looked into. Liam was Doug. The incredulity expanded as Brian finished his regression and stated that this was our current life, yet I had flown into the past with all the smells, visions, feeling, and experiences of the Celtic hills and fires.

Yes, you may be thinking I am completely crazy stating that the woman I saw in the mirror was the one who was described by these five individuals and the regression I had was mere "bit of unprocessed meat" as Scrooge would say. Yet this felt true and real. I certainly wouldn't share it unless I did. People already view me as strange because of the accent. Let's add a past life regression experience to finish the coup! I have described this story in greater detail to my daughter Megan who is writing the story of Callie and Liam as I described it and chance meetings throughout time.

My blindfolded horseback journey continued to the Horse Ancestors through a thin veiled place and I am handed a bone, I am instructed to speak, speak for the horses. My speaking is a gift I must gather and share wherever and whenever I can. This message is an echo of one I had received in a craniosacral treatment. "Speak speak speak speak! Let the river flow. You will speak for us in due time. Ezekiel." The words "ne obliviscaris", Do Not Forget; was forged within my mind as a prayer.

We were asked to make a spirit shield that represented our journey. I drew a Celtic cross with the words "ne obliviscaris", which is the Campbell motto meaning "Do not Forget", God's name and a black horse at the bottom that Megan drew for me. One she was uncertain she could draw, as she didn't feel she was an artist, but it came out beautifully as I had envisioned it. All of these symbols resonated deeply with me and yet it was only when I stepped onto the sand of Iona in Scotland that the feeling of truly being home rose within me.

Chapter 11

THE RETURN HOME

Megan had been accepted to Herstmonceux castle in England for her first year of University in September of 2010. This was a mere year after my accident and she was only 17 and so my mind raced with all of the hesitations any mother would feel. Yet I could not hold her back from this experience. She had worked hard to be accepted and I had to let her go to experience her grand adventure.

Doug and I went with her to the airport. She was flying to England and we were flying to Scotland but would meet her within the week at the castle to see her place of residence for the next year. Our trip to Scotland was also to speak with a reporter, Tracey Bryce, who learned of my accent and accident and wanted to interview me. Well, at least that gave us a good excuse to go in addition to wanting to ensure Megan would be settled at the university! The interview was fun, especially when speaking with someone with a native Scottish accent. I will admit feeling uncomfortable and a bit of a fraud because my accent was claimed through a bump on the head, yet everyone there was comfortable with it and said it was likely from the highlands of Scotland, which, as I said earlier, was confirmed in Inverness while booking a bed and breakfast.

It was a wonderful journey for Doug and me and we mutually agreed that the history and half dilapidated castles were our love. We stood in the Castle of Kilchurn looking over Loch Awe and directly across from it Doug saw a resort that looked exactly like one I had cut out years ago for my "vision board". A vision board is one that you can attach photos to which assist you in envisioning what you dream of having or doing or experiencing. I had always wanted to go to Scotland and so I had attached a photo to state my intention to God and the universe that I wanted to go. This had come to fruition, but who could have predicted that we would stand at the top of Kilchurn castle and see a bed and breakfast so similar to the one I had posted on my wall at home.

I told Doug that we should just sell everything and move here. To which he responded, "First, you can't get the horses across the great pond without a lot of expense. Secondly, to run a bed and breakfast you need to cook and you don't like to do that, and third you would have to do laundry, make beds, clean, garden, and ensure the house was well kept, and that certainly is nothing you like to do." He was right, and so I just enjoyed the view and sent a wee prayer that someday we would return.

Yet as much as Kilchurn castle and Loch Awe resonated with me it was the Isle of Iona that touched my heart and very soul. Walking onto the Island I felt a wave of familiarity. I immediately walked to the bookstore on the Island, as I knew that I would want one from the Isle and they would have books on Celtic liturgy and the history of the Island. Doug wandered the Isle while I found the cherished books I wanted and then we bought the ticket to go into the church. It was upon entering the gate that I felt tears streaming down my face. I could not explain to Doug why I was so emotional, except that it felt like a homecoming to me. It felt like where I began, where I belonged, and to which I was to return and I prayed to never leave.

My body felt illumined and energized. We explored the grounds and too soon our adventure was over. Yet just prior to getting on the boat Doug took a baggy and scooped a small amount of Iona sand into his pocket. (Ok so likely now we will get arrested!) I distributed the sand over our outdoor labyrinth and within my sand labyrinth and when I walk it I not only have the memory, but an embodiment of my connection home. It was a First Nations friend, Cecil, who came for an interaction with our horses who explained the connection to our roots forever resides within us and we are dissatisfied until we step upon them again.

Linda Kohanov in her book, *The Tao of Equus*, explained this connection to our ancestral origins from the work of Rupert Sheldrick. Without delving into this too deeply, and to avoid a bashing for assuming scientific knowledge that is not my forte and certainly admittedly limited understanding, let me just reference his work which he has indicated is similar to Jung's idea of the collective unconscious. Sheldrick does not limit this to humans only, but this permeates through the entire universe. An example of morphic resonance can be seen in our ritual acts which we perform that are similar to those of our ancestors. This is what my native friend was referring to as we evoke the memory in a deliberate and conscious memory back to our roots. Sheldrick feels that these rituals may literally be connecting us to our ancestors (in some sense) through morphic resonance. Paradigms, as mentioned previously, include those that are endemic in our culture that become part of our unconscious and so deeply planted within that we carry on the paradigm, the ingrained ritual even if it is detrimental or limiting in our lives. I believe the horses assist us to gain insight into these paradigms that may be negatively impact us as lasting morphic memories. "A view of paradigms as morphic fields helps us to understand why they are so strongly conserved in nature, for once the paradigms are established, there is a large social group contributing to the consensual reality of the paradigm. A very powerful morphic resonance is evolved by this way of doing things; and that is why paradigm changes tend to be rather rare, and why they meet with strong resistance."[4]

Ok so a long, perhaps convoluted explanation, to try to validate why I felt this deep longing to remain on Iona. Yet this also relates to the horses and the teachings that I would soon become so involved with and adopt right into my very fiber. Linda in her book draws upon the *The Field*, by Kim McTaggart that humans and other living beings are not distinct and separate objects but a coalescence of energy within a larger field of energy, which connects everything within this world.

With this assurance that we are all connected, I returned to Canada knowing that we were never truly apart in this resonance we share. So off to our home in Canada we would return after ensuring Megan was safe and sound within her castle dorm and amidst tears of joy and sorrow to leave her at a destination so far from home. However, I would return to England in February as Megan had an appendicitis attack. Initially when I was called regarding this I was assured that she would have a small incision and since she had already been under anesthetic for a broken arm and wrist two years prior to this, I felt assured that she would pull through without a hitch. However, as I sat at my table talking to Virginia, a beautiful soul who entered into our lives through the horses and now works with me with the horses to share in the horse teachings, I received a call from Megan's emergency contact person in England. God-incidentally enough, Elizabeth is originally from a small town only seven minutes away and was living at the castle at the time of Megan's attendance.

---

4   (http://www.sheldrake.org/Articles&Papers/papers/morphic/morphic2_paper.html).

Elizabeth called on a Thursday morning at 11 a.m. our time, to tell me that Megan was "going back into theatre", which meant surgery for a second time, as she was passing out and there was an accumulation of fluid in her "gut". The fear that went through my body was like a shiver of icy cold wind. What had happened? Had they nicked the bowel and we would have months of healing? Would they be able to correct what had apparently gone very wrong? I give thanks that Virginia was sitting in my kitchen when we received this call. My emotions and inability to truly process what was to be done lulled me to an unmovable paralysis. Yet I looked to Virginia and said, "What should I do?" This began a step by step process with her encouragement and input as I contacted Doug, asked my sister Sandra, who is also a nurse as well, what she felt could have happened and booked a flight to England at 11 p.m.

We made notes to help me to remember important tasks I needed to remember for my well-being in England. And so the Canadian mother with the Scottish accent stood beside her daughter's bed at 3 p.m. in Brighton England time the next day. It was amusing to the doctors and nurses that would continually ask if I had come back home after being in Canada for a time because of the accent. This trip was a huge accomplishment for me. The steps that Virginia and I were able to lay out, I followed and although I was exhausted by the time I arrived, I was able to be with Megan as she recovered from her second surgery, which was a result of internal bleeding.

Once again tears streamed down my face as I left Megan to return home. I also returned to the Horse Spirit Connections hoping to learn more of equine facilitation and hopefully begin a new journey with my own horses. Wendy and Andre invited me to their home to participate in their FEEL (Facilitated Equine Experiential Learning) Program as a healing journey. The first day was a balance of being with the group and going to the house to rest. Wendy helped me to understand that self-care was necessary to enable me to care for and have compassion for others. However, regardless of this theory, I still experienced another life altering health experience that found me whisked away in an ambulance from their retreat centre.

Chapter 12

COFFEE AND CARE

The second morning at the Horse Spirit Connections Centre FEEL Training I arose to find no one in the house. I stepped into the kitchen to make a pot of coffee. I took the pot and rinsed it beneath the water only to have it crack. What a way to start a day! I have a sign on my fridge "There are only two rules in the morning. Rule #1 Don't talk to me until I have had my coffee. Rule #2 Don't talk to me until I have had my coffee." I also have a sign from a friend "I don't think there is enough coffee in my coffee stream." And my sister gave me a jar to hold my coffee in and it says, "Everyone has to believe in something. I believe I'll have another coffee." So you can see what breaking this pot signified to me—an emergency! I truly felt that I could only go out to greet the others after I had my coffee. Yet I quietly squeezed myself around the gathering people out in the retreat centre who had already arrived to begin the second day to get a cup of coffee from the carafe. "Thanks be to God" was my feeling! Second hurtle, sharing with the group, but at least I had a coffee!

We were told to go and check in with the horses and it was not until I went to see Monty, a horse that wore a cribbing collar for the habit of locking his teeth onto the wood and sucking in a gulp of air, which is defined as cribbing. As I looked at him standing in the stall with the crib collar on, two things occurred to me. First, although he had an addiction, he was still a contributing member of the herd. It helped me to realize that although I had the brain injury, I too could be a contributing member of my family. It gave me a sense of relief and a renewed purpose that I could adapt myself to the "new" me and learn to be purposeful in this.

Second, I was addicted to coffee. Um – no shit Sherlock! Lord love a duck! How much coffee was too much? And from all the studies you could choose whatever statistic you wanted to make it a vice or a plus. As in most studies, there are controversial issues. In that moment however, the light bulb had gone on bright and clear. Maybe I should cut back on my coffee? I would only drink a full carafe in the first hour of my day. Too much you think? I guess right?

At that moment of brilliant enlightenment I headed to the house but not before Thor reached out and touched my trapezes muscle— the one between the neck and shoulder joint. Mine is always so tight I laugh and say I look like a Cardassian from Star Trek. My right one is always the tightest, but when Thor touched it, I felt it snap like an elastic band. I rubbed it and moved my neck around to decrease the tension.

As I continued to head to the house for lunch I began dragging my left leg. This didn't alarm me, as on occasion after the back surgery I would experience numbness in my feet and a wee bit of instability in my leg. I had lunch, of course never mentioning to anyone this feeling, and headed out to begin the next experience. Yet I knew something was wrong. Not quite sure what it was but something was going sideways again!

I watched the next participant interact with the horse in the round pen but had to get up and leave the arena feeling dizzy and weak. Over time it was decided that I should go to the hospital and before the ambulance arrived I had lost feeling on my left side and was becoming increasingly confused and overwhelmed by the gathering paramedics and concerned onlookers.

Once again I journeyed to the hospital in the ambulance with sirens blaring. I was rushed past everyone waiting in the lobby and taken into the emergency room. I could not lift my left arm and had lost feeling in the left leg, as well as, my ability to speak eluded me again. This was very scary as I couldn't answer the questions being asked of me and I only knew Wendy from the workshops so she really did not know my medical history to share with them.

I had a tongue depressor lunged to the back of my throat with no gag reaction present, the doctor assumed it was a lower brainstem problem and they advanced with great caution. The symptoms lasted 24 hours and then slowly all movement and speech returned. I was told it was likely a TIA (trans ischemic attack)—a small stroke and to follow up with my doctor.

Again poor Doug was phoned and told that I had been taken to hospital by ambulance, but this time he had to travel four hours to get to the hospital. I am sure those were four long hours and I said to him, in broken stuttering words as he stood at the end of my bed "We need to stop meeting like this!" I was released after a two night stay. Once again I returned to my bedroom tired, disenchanted, angry, and fearful. It seemed that my life was to be restricted physically, mentally, and even when I chose to step out of my cocooned space I would be overwhelmed or worse, challenged with a health concern that limited me. And to make matters even more harrowing—I was told to quit drinking coffee! I did this cold turkey and I still can't figure why our favourite coffee distributor,

Tim Horton's, didn't go bankrupt in the time I wasn't drinking their coffee!

I am sure that you have realized my tenacity by now. I would again and again try to journey through the FEEL program with the horses at Wendy and Andre's as I felt that they were healing and making me feel whole again. One of the changes that many would see upon my return from the Horse Spirit Connections was a decreased amount of stuttering in my speech. I would be more relaxed, confident, and felt purposeful again in my new direction with my horses.

I was purposeful—not purpose-full. What is the difference you ask? I had found purpose again but not so much so that I was running here and there and creating anxiety, frustration, and health concerns. I would balance rest with my time with the horses. This new purpose of just "being" with the horses I was able to once again feel useful and worthy.

Chapter 13
FALLING INTO SOMEONE NEW

*A*fter struggling with my new reality for three years, I'd finally had enough—enough of feeling frustrated, enough of feeling isolated, and enough of being unable to cope with day-to-day life. So over the next few years, I researched and tested a multitude of traditional and non-traditional therapeutic coping strategies, until I devised a holistic routine that provided me with the relief I was desperately seeking.

And slowly, but surely, I emerged from my cocoon state and rejoined the world—born anew.

I vowed to start a routine that would allow me to focus and learn to adapt and regain as much of the pre-fall person as I could. It would be a struggle that I would continue to invest in even though it was impossible to become the "super woman" I had been. I would often say to Doug that I don't know who that woman was or how he put up with her.

As such, each morning, after Doug had gone to work and the girls had left for school, I would sit in my bed, sip tea (still no coffee!), meditate, and pray. I know it may seem odd to do this before even experiencing any challenges in my day, but I was preparing myself for the inevitable. There is no one that is free from stress. At least "not until the undertaker undertakes to take you under"! So, I prayed daily and gave thanks for even the smallest of gains that I had made, and I asked for the fortitude, hope, and optimism I needed to greet each day.

A prayer of gratitude is simple and yet profound in helping to shift us from the negativity that we seem to so readily adopt and helps to balance the rhythm of co-joining the heart, brain, and the rest of the body in love. It has been proven that expressing gratitude helps us to be healthier, happier, and feel more fulfilled. Yet, my prayer wouldn't end there. I would carry "it" throughout my day to help me stay focused, centered, and calm. This of course didn't always lead to success, but I was looking for improvement, not perfection.

Later in my day, I may walk the labyrinth that I spoke of earlier that is in our backyard. The labyrinth is a walking meditation that weaves you to its center and back out again on the same path, so truly where it ends—it begins. The labyrinth isn't meant to confuse or frustrate you. In the labyrinth, you do not lose yourself. In the labyrinth, you are found.

How did we come to make this decision to put a 52' helicopter landing pad in our back yard? Pre-accident (a lot of my time line is based on "Pre-accident" or "Post-accident") as I was completing my Master's in Divinity I was a part of a group of women in Ministry. I shared with them my difficulty in being able to stay still and focused in prayer and meditation. The "itty bitty shitty committee" – the bully within - would begin to announce itself, or I would begin to think of all the duties and tasks I had to do or I would just feel like jumping up. My friend Cheryl suggested that I should try a labyrinth, which combined movement and meditation.

I must admit the first time I walked one I was self-conscious, restless, and just couldn't understand what was truly required. Of course the pre-accident person I was had to know why it worked, was it reasonable, logical and what was the purpose and science of just walking around a big circle? My left-brain dominance just couldn't comprehend the reason for doing this. However, now my intuitive sensing creative brain loves this activity!

The sensible person I was then however, felt I needed to do a five-day labyrinth training to "really get it." So I went off to train with the Rev. Dr. Lauren Artress who had resurrected it from the Chartres Cathedral in France. I discovered that labyrinths had been found in many cultures all over the world. They were found on tables, coins, pottery, and hillsides as far back as 5,000 years. They have been used in numerous way—to promote well-being, inner peace, a way to clear the mind and focus attention, a place to take a "time out" to reflect upon choices or directions in your life, and a place to regain clarity and balance. Labyrinths have been found to decrease stress, quiet the mind and open the heart to possibilities in a calm focused centre. Research has been done regarding the positive effects of labyrinths for neurological reasons as well. The four-quadrant path balances the hemispheres and has been shown to increase mental clarity. Yet it is nothing didactic. Each time you walk it you discover something new or you just find peace and quiet within your day.

How to "walk" a finger labyrinth -

1. Find a quiet spot and sit in a comfortable position.
2. Place your finger labyrinth in front of you.
3. Enter the labyrinth with the forefinger of your nondominant hand. (If using your non-dominant hand is awkward or uncomfortable, use the forefinger of your dominant hand instead.)
4. Trace the pattern of the labyrinth with your finger. Clear your mind of extraneous thoughts and focus solely on following the path.
5. "Walk" to the center of the labyrinth and then rest/pause momentarily. Notice if your mental chatter has become quiet and if you have a sense of well being.
6. "Walk" out of the labyrinth. Then take a deep relaxing **breath.**

I have found that each time I walk the labyrinth it is different. Of course, I AM different each time and at times I walk it alone or in a group. While walking as a group you will find that you come face to face with someone walking in as you are walking out. I find this to be very symbolic of life as we cross paths with others, not I believe by accident, there is an intention or reason behind each encounter. Within the labyrinth there are short paths turn and longer paths before you turn. It will take you close to the heart of the labyrinth, the centre of the Chartres Labyrinth being the Rose of Sharon, and then to the outer edges. I found this to be symbolic as well since we often feel we have got to the centre, to the prize, before we have barely begun. I often felt that I had reached the goal only to find myself on the edge of something new.

I learned within the labyrinth that I am a creator, not a finisher. I love to create but I often walk away form a project when it is at its height of success. The fun will pass and the monotony of maintaining it creates a longing within me to begin something new. Post-accident I have truly actualized this and find myself finding peace and joy in the monotony of cutting grass, cleaning stalls, maintaining the labyrinth and so on. The chores on a farm are endless. You will never complete them, but I now find more contentment in this cycle of care.

Reaching the centre is really only half the journey, the returning journey to the outside world is the completion. In the labyrinth I acquired a tune that I have asked many to identify but have found no one who has been able to. I feel it is my own sacred song of connection. Music really is the connection and emotion that we cannot see but we feel deeply.

Upon my return from the labyrinth workshop I did a retreat day for the ministers of the United Church of Canada. I had purchased a 25' canvas labyrinth that I could take to various places to introduce them to the labyrinth. Doug videotaped this retreat day as I was gaining a master's credit for my work with the labyrinth. Upon rising on Sunday morning, I found Doug at the kitchen table with grid paper and pencil in hand. He had drawn a retreat area of 2 acres of ponds, walking paths, trees, gazebo, and bushes with a large labyrinth at the heart of it. He knew before I did what potential a labyrinth would have to bring peace to our family, the community, and to those who travel by the air ambulance helicopter on its way to London from Chatham with silent prayers following from the labyrinth.

The labyrinth was not just our project. It became a community project because we invited as many people as possible from the community to come and place a brick onto the site. We had a couple from Kentucky come to lay out the pattern, as you would guess, I wanted it to be perfect in proportion and design. The project began with the couple being stopped at the US/Canadian border. After much ado Stuart and Mary were finally able to arrive at the farm and design the centre. We finished the full pattern 24 hours later and they said it was the easiest labyrinths they had laid down.

Unfortunately that day we couldn't complete it fully but it didn't stop the kids from running through it and trying to follow the pattern. Once it was completed we invited our neighbors and friends to return to the "labyrinth christening" ceremony. Karen Price, who had become a fast friend at the labyrinth workshop, had given me a bottle of water that she had brought from the Jordan River. We took this and mixed it with water from our farm, put it in Dixie cups and while I taught the adults about the labyrinth and its purpose, the kids and the dogs walked the labyrinth and poured the water from the Dixie cups throughout the path. You would think this would have become a water fight for sure, yet the kids quietly, with seriousness of intention, poured the water on the labyrinth ensuring each inch was christened.

Walking the labyrinth helped me to quiet that left-brain nattering with all its criticism. Finding the time to focus on this type of self-care is scarce with the number of roles we play. Yet life is too short not to find the time to take care of ourselves and spend our sacred time with family and friends rather than so focused on work and materialism.

I know the old adage, "Life is too short." is overused, but I wrote the book *Creating from Within Harmony* before my accident, based on this idea. It's funny how I was unable to recognize this message in my daily life at the time. I lectured and emphasized chapter after chapter, about the importance of creating "faith, hope, and a celebration of life in this 'hurry-up' world," yet I continued to race against time as though I could reclaim the lost moments with my children and correct my health concerns effortlessly. But it wasn't until after my accident that I *really* lived the truths that I wrote about in the book. And yes, now I have time to meditate, pray, exercise, and sleep, but this freedom came about by a life changing event and it carries with it challenges and trade-offs that I would not have chosen on my own.

The increased focus and pruning of activities that I had to make (to accommodate the person I had become) helped me realize that my greatest desire was the ability to spend time with my family. Not just time, but real and focused time; being fully present—mind, body, and soul.

My daughter, Megan, said to me this summer—"Mom, it was the first time you have been in the pool in three years!" It was hard to swim with a computer on my lap, the phone to my ear, and reading a book for my Masters courses. But now, I have received the gift of focus and being truly present with those I love. Malachi, my horse, helped me to actualize this. He has taught me to stay in the present moment, for that is the only time that is truly real.

As for my other post-concussion symptoms, I don't really see them as gifts, per se—even after five years, I am still sensitive to light and sound. I work very hard to adjust to this but I still find stores too bright, too crowded, and make it difficult to do things such as grocery shopping. Yet I am very lucky as Doug does this. This has been our agreement since our first year of marriage when I returned home one day from the grocery store complaining that elderly people should shop on any days except the weekend because it was the only time I had to get groceries. He responded, "Well perhaps it is the only way they get social interaction?" Upon which I said, "You are too nice. You can do it from now on." And he has.

Doug also used to do the laundry. Again this is a result of an agreement we had. I wanted our washer and dryer up on the main living area rather than in the lower level so I wasn't carrying baskets up and down the stairs. Doug however, wanted the set in the basement and so I stated that as long as the washer and dryer were downstairs he could do the laundry. However, after my accident the washer and dryer were moved upstairs and I began to do the laundry. This was the only thing that I could do that made me feel like I was able to complete something. Yet I would be doing laundry and someone would come in and switch the finished wash to the dryer. This may appear helpful but it only confused me because I couldn't remember if I did it or if someone else changed it. This would leave me angry and frustrated so I enacted a rule that if the laundry room light was on I was doing laundry and no one was to touch it. I still keep the light on if I am doing laundry to this day.

Since my accident, I've had to institute a number of cues to remind myself of the things I should be doing. I create a daily schedule using the calendar app on my iPhone and I set audio reminders that alert me of upcoming appointments and meetings. In the beginning, I even included basic events like eating and napping.

Not only do the reminders help me remember what I have to do, but they also allow me to set the maximum time I want to dedicate to a task so I don't get overtired or frustrated. I would truly be lost without my iPhone. It even contains "brain games", like Diner Dash, Suduko, and Yhatsee, that help improve my decision-making and processing abilities. No waiting for a table at my diner!

Before the fall, I played both the guitar and violin. Afterward, I could remember chords, but not strum rhythmically or combine singing with it. However, I do remember the day I could combine these. It was after I attended a parishioner's funeral. I was feeling unsteady, so I decided to return home rather than attend the graveside service and luncheon. When I got home I picked up my guitar to play and sing two favorite hymns of the lady whose funeral I had just attended. It seemed as if I had never forgotten how to play the guitar. The plasticity of the brain is a miracle. My playing the guitar is a clear example of why anyone who has suffered a brain trauma should remain hopeful and never give up trying. I continue to try to play the violin as well, knowing that music is helpful to my recovery.

I still have trouble regulating my emotions. When my "emotional chip" is activated—watch out! I not only feel emotion deeply, but passionately, and it comes on fast and furious. These extreme emotional fluctuations have been some of the most challenging struggles for me and contribute to my anxiety and feelings of being overwhelmed.

I'm still sensitive to the feelings of those around me, and get the "wobbles", from time to time. However, working with the horses, which I will talk about has helped me become grounded, aware of my body, and aware of what I am feeling—without taking on the emotions of others.

Chapter 14

LEARNING TO DRIVE

I love to drive our team of horses, my Fjords—Brad and Bill, dressed in full uniform—a vest, helmet, and carrot stick (a Parelli stick for communication). I looked like a Knight from King Arthur's court! As I mentioned previously, my processing speed had gone from about 150% to 10% which is why Dr. Saudia Ahmad, my neuropsychologist, diagnosed me as "completely disabled", and told me she would rather I didn't drive a car. So, I have had to work at training myself to make decisions and think quickly but behind the wheel of a car wasn't such a great idea. But I tell you, nothing quite forces you to process quickly and make a decision than when you are driving a team of horses through a woodlot. You can hear me yell "Billy–Gee–look out for that tree!" It has taken time and practice to remember that Bill is Gee—which means when I give that command I want the team to turn right, and Brad–Haw—which means I want to turn to the left. Yet they are forgiving creatures and innately know when to just lead because the lady at the reins can't decide quickly enough.

It was Brad and Bill, my team of Fjords that pulled a wagon for me and who taught me to drive a car again. Megan was in the process of getting her license and driving for the first time and I could understand the feelings she felt of heightened awareness and uncertainty, yet I know she was excited to get behind the wheel. Me on the other hand . . . not so much.

I used to love to drive. I was confident, relaxed, and would drive anywhere. It relaxed me, and to be honest, I could write a sermon, yes literally write notes while I drove. (I no longer do this!) Now however, I felt awkward, anxious, and hyperconscious.

Dr Ahmad suggested to me that we should have someone throw a ball out in front of the car to practice my driving skills and ability to react quickly. I had already restricted my driving to necessary runs, which I would do first thing in the morning, as often as I could, because this was when I was the most alert. Driving later in the day often resulted in more difficulty speaking and hampered my processing, and often resulted in dizziness, nausea, and a headache.

The doctor also instructed us that when retraining the brain do not let the brain get overtired. The brain could change or adapt again through the process of neuroplasticity, which is "the brain's ability to reorganize itself by forming new neural connections. Neuroplasticity allows the neurons (nerve cells) in the brain to compensate for injury and disease and to adjust their activities in response to new situations or to changes in their environment."[5] The brain could compensate for the damage by forming new connections to deal with new activities. Yet you should not cross the line. In other words, if I began to tire doing an activity in ten minutes, I should stop the activity in eight to nine minutes rather than trying to continue on and overtax the brain. This is why pacing, not overdoing it, is so important.

---

5   http://www.medterms.com/script/main/art.asp?articlekey=40362

So how do I learn to drive again when my processing has diminished to ten percent of normal without endangering others? I hitch up the team of Fjord horses I purchased before my fall and drive them through the woodlot. A bit unconventional I know, and I am sure it would be difficult for most people to find a team of horses to take out into the bush, but that really was how I recovered my driving skills and practiced making decisions.

My friend Lana would come down and we would hitch up the boys, Brad and Bill. This alone was an exercise in neuroplasticity as I tried to untangle the harness and clip on all the essential parts. Remember, I bought these horses only two months prior to my accident so I had never harnessed horses nor driven a team before. That was "Pre-fall Sharon" who had confidence, strength, and tenacity. "Post-fall Sharon" became frustrated easily, overwhelmed quickly, and physically tired within a short period of doing anything. So this new learning pushed a number of buttons and edges.

Once we got into the bush and the speed picked up it became necessary to direct them faster and faster and you had to say their names, which I couldn't remember that quickly. We certainly had some close calls. I would mix up names and directions but my co-pilot Lana would never get excited and grab the reins. She would just laugh and yell out the right command. I have never had so much fun with learning a new skill in all my life. Only once did I run Brad into a two-inch sapling! But he remained calm and I was able to get him to back up and off we would go again.

I was eventually able to harness the boys, always with Lana's help, and take them out driving with confidence, joy, and feeling empowered that I was able to accomplish this new task. It was exhausting and exhilarating all at the same time! And it really did help me to process faster, make quick decisions, and access my memory to accomplish the task.

As I write this today Bill has just passed away suddenly from a small intestinal tumor or blockage. It seems impossible because in his last two weeks he had chosen to participate in the equine therapy three times. I rarely use either of the Fjord horses for the teaching unless I was trying to highlight how a team can work together so well because they don't like to be separated in the stalls for the program. They were always together. Yet in his last days Bill taught a lesson of kind compassionate and quiet leadership to a leader of a health agency—authenticity to a fellow who was having difficulty being present in the moment and how to speak up and call for help rather than go it alone for another.

Brad of course is now without his teammate Bill. He has the other members of the herd but it really was he and Bill who spent 95% of their time together. When Bill passed we brought Brad in to be with him and have time to see Bill in his inert presence and allow the mourning to begin. After all we are a people of meaning, regardless if it is a horse or a person that we share this sacred journey with.

I have a friend who has told me numerous times that she does not want a funeral upon her passing. No visitation, no graveside service, and certainly no dinner. To which I always reply, "Well it's not all about you. And by that time you won't be able to stop me!" to which we laugh. A funeral is not just about the person that has died. Oh yes we share stories and memories, scriptures and songs that the person enjoyed and which define him or her as the person we loved. Yet the funeral process truly is about those who gather together and share in the memories. Those who need to find joy, meaning, and hope without that individual to share in their lives. It is filling the space that has been created with past memories of their dear friend or family member, and then gently, compassionately, with great love they begin that day to create new and beautiful memories.

I went to the house to lay down after leaving Brad in the stall with Bill but I felt unsettled so I went back to stand by the stall that they were in. Brad looked to me, walked over, breathed into my nostrils, looked back at the body of Bill, breathed deeply and then pounded his hoof upon the stall door as if to say, "I am done." Once we had buried Bill's remains I brought Brad back to see the empty stall so he could perhaps understand that Bill truly has transitioned. Yet for Brad there will be many firsts. The first time we bring him into the barn without Bill to trim his mane and the first time I put on the harness but he will not have Bill beside him to ground and guide him throughout his job of safely pulling the cart for me and the others who I would often convince to come on my outings.

I can't help but see these firsts as similar to those that have lost loved ones and they experience their first Christmas without their friend or family member, or the first birthday, your own and the loved ones that passes. I recall my first birthday after my mom had passed. Standing looking out of the sliding glass door and thinking that she had given me life and now her life had been taken. It was a strange feeling.

For me deep meaning and a change in my life occurred with that loss. It was only a couple of weeks after my daughter's baptism and her birthday that my mother suddenly died of lobar pneumonia. It was a loss in which I found myself shaken. I had always felt in control and had never truly battled with my faith and death. How funny—every day we are dying but we ignore it until our death—and then it is too late. Yet is it?

On rare occasions I will share with individuals the experiences I have witnessed from a sleep like state or in a shifting of reality and non-reality in which I have felt the presence of those that have gone before me. My mother shared with me, in a dreamlike state while I received a craniosacral treatment that "Where it ends . . . it begins." How true for so many events in life. The loss of a job can make opportunities you would never have known if you remained in the previous employment. An ended relationship may lead to an expanded family that you would never have had the chance to know and love. A loss of a loved one, in which we search for meaning and hope, perhaps opens us to being the strength, hope, and witness to another in their time of loss.

Death, loss, and uninitiated change all manifest in us the discomfort of what we feel as loss of control. We experience fear, uncertainty, and isolation. A sense that no one truly understands what we are going through, which is true to an extent, for it is unique to you within its meaning and relevance, but we are truly never totally alone. In my journey to the dark abode of my bedroom, I had a choice to reach out to my family, to my friends, to the horses, and to further medical and psychological help and to share the teachings of the horses with others rather than never expressing them because others would think I was weird, illogical, or had completely lost it.

For years I have shared with individuals only what I have felt they wanted to hear and tried to be the person they wanted to see. Yet Bill's passing has encouraged me to step up and speak, write, and teach, which has always been my true gift, or area of genius as Gay Hendricks refers to it. Before burying Bill, my friend Lana and I trimmed off his tail. It was something that we both felt strongly about and we laughed that people would think that we were nuts. Regardless, we washed it, braided it, put beautiful ribbons through it and made it an exhibit to honor Bill and to the generation of horses before him and to follow. Later Lana found it written that by conserving the horse's tail, you are transferring to the horse's owner, the horse's spirit. I truly believe that Bill has shared and enlivened me with his spirit of leadership, authenticity, communication skills to work well with others, and an ability to take the lead while teaching others.

Part Two

MESSAGES STRAIGHT FROM THE HORSE'S MOUTH

"The outside of the horse is good for the inside of a person."
—Winston Churchill

*M*ost people react the same way when they find out that Malachi and I have a great relationship and I even occasionally ride him: "How could you still ride that horse when he caused your accident in the first place?"

Although it may seem weird to those of you reading this, it turns out that the very thing that caused my "great fall" is the very thing that helped me recover from it. My herd of horses truly healed me by their quiet abiding presence. I had learned from my interactions with the horses at Wendy and Andre's how to just be with them and allow my anxiety, fears, and self-recrimination to ease and fade while I was just out watching and relaxing with these majestic beings.

They made no judgments, they didn't care that I knew not what I wanted to do in the future, they had no interest in my bank account, they weren't checking the time to see how long I had been out with them, and as I tired they were never critical of the fact that I would need to go lie down. Quite the opposite. They were teaching me to reject the obstacles imposed by my human society and experience a new way of being in a new community—their community.

Virginia, whom I mention earlier, was the only person who would enter into this abiding presence with the horses. A mutual acquaintance had asked if she could bring a few people out to walk the labyrinth. It was a last minute request and I was busy with Lana hitching Brad and Bill, our Fjord team, up to go for another adventure, but I felt that it would not interfere if they just went to the labyrinth in the back to walk. I was wrong about this. I had not as yet come to realize how the presence of others would affect me. Although I wanted to be gracious, the interruption to share in their arrival and departure affected my ability to focus and relax while harnessing the boys. Brad would be my indicator of rising frustration, anxiety, and agitation, as he would move away from the harness and me when I started to experience this. And that day he would not stand still!

This however gave Virginia an opportunity to see the labyrinth and the facilities and she would pass on to our area hospital, who was doing staff training, that our place would be a great retreat and teaching area away from the formal hospital training centre. Leaders brought 20 individuals per day over a two-day period to experience the labyrinth and our retreat area. I agreed to this because all that was expected of me was to put out coffee and a lunch, which Doug purchased—prepackaged from a catering service.

As people arrived I would fade into the background and go out to be with the horses once the coffee was on. Then, one of the leaders asked if I could sit with them and introduce myself, and the labyrinth, to the participants. I felt a rise of panic and fear at this request, but again, trying to be graceful and accommodating I agreed to stay. Yet what started as an introduction turned into leading of a walk through the labyrinth. It did spark a bit of anxiety but because the activity was a quiet one, I did not feel overwhelmed.

After introducing the facilities and the labyrinth I made my exit and headed to the house to rest until I was needed for the lunch. Just before leaving I told them I would open one of the gates so that the horses could come up closer and they could pet them and be in their presence. I did not know however that when I allowed the horses access to the paddock where they could be seen easier that I had forgotten a gate on a previous occasion and this would let all ten of them out to roam free.

Sounds lovely doesn't it that they could just roam the property. And it was lovely as the participants would share with me later. During their break they went out and interacted with the horses who were by this time walking around the labyrinth and the retreat area free to eat the grass. Participants commented to each other how lovely it was that I would just let them wander amongst the horses and how calm the horses were. There were a few individuals that questioned how we kept them restricted to this area but I had said I was going to let them out so they could interact with them and they thought I really wanted this to happen.

The horses remained wandering the property when the participants and leaders went back to continue with their course. At noon I would walk down to set out the food only to realize that the horses were out. I went into the building for a minute to report that the horses were out and I was going to round them up and off I went to bring them in.

Horses, as I shared in my experience with the energy round pen, sense right away the emotion and energy level of people. They had previously got out to wander the property but I always had Doug or Megan to assist me. My friend Lana had come to help but it soon became obvious that we were a little anxious about what was going on and that energy was passed on to the horses. To the horses (being prey animals), Lana and I looked and acted like predators. What should have been an easy job of throwing ropes over their backs and bringing them in turned into a full out stampede.

When Lana and I went to the back yard two or three of the more sensitive horses immediately lifted their heads. I could sense their very breath and rising anxiety but at this point I had not learned to flow with the emotion by checking in with it and using strategies to cope and calm the situation. So, when we walked to the back the rising heads soon turned into horses darting around and off to the bush behind our property. We had a laneway of grass so they stayed to that area as they headed out and I jumped on our golf cart to assist in bringing them back.

We caught up with them about half way back and Lana and I would jump off the golf cart to throw ropes over a few of them to help us bring them back to the barn. This was all going swimmingly until Lana walked past the golf cart with Malachi and he spied a bag of carrots that I was bringing down to the group for lunch. Lana said it was the funniest thing she had ever seen. He started to go by the golf cart with her and then he took a double take and grabbed the carrots with his mouth. He shook the bag causing carrots to fly everywhere, which spooked the already anxious horses around him and caused them to take off again. I barely heard or understood what Lana said but I knew enough to let go of the two horses I had rather than pull a shoulder out or get dragged by them.

Off they went again and back to the golf cart we would go to catch up to them. It was thundering hooves that the participants at the retreat center heard and a few heads poked out to see what was going on. I left the slow golf cart to switch to a faster mode of transportation, the four-wheeler. Some of the folks asked if they could help so I asked a group of them to stand at the end of the laneway and block the horses when I brought them back. I had another group stand at the other end of the lane and wave their arms to encourage the horses to go to the paddock gate. A third group was to help funnel them through the gate into their paddock.

It all seemed to happen in a second and off down the field I roared to catch up to the horses who were galloping down the field parallel to the road and heading toward a busy highway. I had to get them turned back. Honestly, I have no idea how all of this got orchestrated but adrenalin and concern for the horses engulfed me as I flew down the field leaving Lana to set everyone up to block them if I could get them turned around. I continued to yell to the horses "Here boys, hey boys, right here boys." I knew that our original three horses, Midnight, Ice, and Kigh would respond to those convincing words that they should return to me. The time I had spent just hanging out and being with them would pay off as these three horses turned and suddenly were running towards me.

I turned the ATV and headed for home. I could feel the energy behind me and was caught up in the excitement and exhilaration as they actually flew by me. The thundering hooves and the beauty took my breath away but incited fear into the individuals who were blocking them from going past the house. I had told them that if they would just wave their arms as a group that the horse would turn from them and head in the direction of the barn. A few afterwards shared that it took great trust to stand there with arms waving as they felt the movement of the ground as ten horses thundered towards them.

Yet they waved in harmony and off to the barn the horses ran to another group of waving individuals who directed them towards the gate and into the paddock. What an exciting and harrowing experience for all involved! But what great fun it was at the same time. This soon turned into laughter and comic retelling of how the fear rose within the participants as the horses drew near but that together they were able to stand steadfast and focus on the task of directing the horses. This was a serendipitous lesson in teamwork for a group that had come to our centre to learn just that. Of course I'm sure the horses must have known this and gave them a real life experience to enhance their day's lesson.

Later I chatted with Virginia, who had been in one of the "hand waving groups" directing the horses back to the barn and God-incidentally as we talked about the horses she shared that she was in a coaching program with a lady who was learning equine therapy. Come to find out in the midst of that conversation, Virginia was speaking of Jean, an individual I had met and had become fast friends with at an equine training event. She had immediately resonated with me and would graciously care and look out for me at the events. Coincidence? I believe there really are no coincidences, but just God-incidences to bring souls together that need to intertwine in the dance of life to learn and teach lessons that we share with one another.

Virginia continued to come back to the farm to visit the horses and ended up learning how to partner with them, to understand them, and to share in their wisdom. She now owns our wee mare Miriam who is the matriarch of the herd. Miriam is the only mother in the herd with her daughter Milcah, and she is the oldest member. She was the one that anyone would choose to ride because of her small size and her lovely disposition to take you anywhere or if she had had enough of the riding arena she would stop dead in the middle to offer you her back as a chair, because she wasn't going anywhere.

Message 1

Remain present to the moment

*H*orses have a natural ability to help us to remain in the present moment. They help us to not judge our past or plan our future so minutely that we miss the present. Without a word, horses affirm our innate worth, demand that we act authentically, and direct us to what is happening now, in the present moment. They do not approach us with any preconceived notions on how we should or should not act. They accept us for who we are, a child of God, a precious child, and worthy of a life full of joy so we can live abundantly and fully, regardless of how society defines us. Every person is unique, gifted, and worthy of joy, hope, and love.

They sense and share with us that it is in the moment of honest, open, quiet, reflection that we truly identify that which we seek—the connection within our hearts to the awakening of the soul. For it is only in this time of silence and solitude that the shy soul peaks out through the façade of a life filled with activity. It is in the stillness and quiet that we can catch a breath, refocus, and be in the presence of the divine, revealed through the horse who can glimpse our soul. Our soul resonates with the authenticity and acceptance that the horses share with us.

I do not believe the accident was accidental. I believe it was an awakening for me, one that tested my beliefs, my faith, and my ability to be open to possibilities and intuitive wisdom that came from my horses, especially Malachi, the messenger of God.

Malachi has taught me to be fully present with the person I am with. Just try to be in the presence of these large gregarious creatures and let your mind wander. They will quickly start to "play" with you making you move with a nudge or a wee nip to see if you are paying attention. It can be quite dangerous to be with a horse but thinking about a project at work. The horses know if you are truly present, focused on them and if you are being authentic.

Horses do not like to be alone. They want and need the socialization of a herd. Yet within their herd they have a pecking order. There is one horse that will be the alpha, then a second, a third, and so on. Brad and Bill were the lowest on the pecking order. It doesn't go by the size of the horse; it is truly a physical, psychological, and non-verbal communication that establishes their hierarchies.

Iceman had always been our alpha until we brought a paint horse named Atlas in. You never put new horses together straight away. You would see the new horse being chased and kicked and everyone at once trying to establish their dominance over him. So we kept Atlas separated by a fence for a time. He could still see the horses over the fence but he was protected. We eventually let them all together and Ice chased Atlas away from the herd. If he came near Iceman would bare his teeth and chase him away. Doug was out in the paddock when he saw the transition in leadership. Ice and Atlas went at it for a minute. Atlas won the contest and then it was over—Atlas had become the leader.

When I was working with Malachi and other horses come up to us, even Atlas as the alpha, I would protect Malachi and not let Atlas near him. If Malachi was drinking from the water trough I ensured that other horses could not get a drink until he was done. I wanted Malachi to know that I was fully present with him, he was safe with me, and he could count on me as his leader.

This translates to our relationships with family and friends. Being present, mind, body, and spirit when you are with another reveals to them that you care, that you are really listening, that you see them as the most important person in your life in that moment. While the girls were in high school, I was home when they arrived home at the end of their day at school because of the accident. I could be doing other things that were on my list of "supposed to do", but I would rather sit at the counter and listen to them talk about their day, the challenges, the fun and Mikayla would get a story going and Meg and I would laugh the whole time. Mikayla really can tell a "story" well. Often their stories made me so proud because they were always for the underdog.

Both of my girls have tattoos. I know I know—some of you reading this are okay with it and some not so much, others never. I actually got a tattoo as well on both my wrists. The left wrist has the Celtic tree of life that Megan has on her ankle, and within it I inscribed Isaiah 49:15-16. For that scripture states, "Can a mother forget the baby at her breast and have no compassion for the child she has borne? Though she may forget, I will not forget you! See, I have engraved you on the palms of my hands" [6]

If God has us tattooed on the palms of his hands I can but do the same and so on my left wrist I have God's name so that I can see it and know whose I truly am. I also have an infinity symbol that Mikayla has on the back of her neck, as this is an endless love. And of course some will argue that Isaiah 49:15-16 is not interpreted this way. It doesn't matter. I support my girls in their tattoos. Mikayla has on her left trapezius—"One Life One Chance" and Megan has in the same place "We are One". To me that speaks volumes of their character and for me,

---

6   The Holy Bible, The New Revised Standard Version, Oxford Press, Anglicized Edition, Oxford University Press 1998.

it links me forever to my girls and to the Lord, The Infinite One, The Great Spirit in our lives.

Oh yes, around the tree of life on my left wrist is written "Ne Obliviscaris" —Do Not Forget—Malachi. And to include Doug I have the Irish Claddah symbol with anam cara, which means soul friend.

Be present. Let your friends and family know you care. You don't have to get a tattoo to do this. The greatest gift you can give someone is your attention.

God's Tattoos

Not in the sky, because the sky is too high
Not in the clouds, because the clouds can't hold you
Not on a stone, for a stone is too cold
Not on silver or gold, lest anyone think you could be sold
Not in a book, because a book could be lost
But on the palms of my hands
On the flesh
Where you can't be lost, sold or forgotten
On the flesh
Where I see you all the time
On the flesh
Where the pain was measured out in love
On the flesh
In the warm, permanent skin of my Son
There you are …
Eternally
Indelibly
Part of me
Engraved

Cut into

At great cost

Scarred forever

As my tattoo

By John Fischer

Strategies to Be fully Present—
To bring awareness to the moment that is NOW
The APB—You know how the police put out an "all-points bulletin" for someone who's been lost? Well this strategy will teach you how to find yourself in the midst of the negative thoughts that are running wild in your mind.

It all starts by checking in with your arousal level. Think of your arousal level as a scale from zero to ten, zero being you are so relaxed you are almost asleep and ten being you can barely think or act because you are so overwhelmed.

To gain awareness of when your arousal level is increasing you will need to stay connected to your thoughts and how your body feels. What does it feel like when you are becoming anxious, frustrated, or overwhelmed? Your body may tense, your breathing may become shallow, and your heart rate may quicken or race. You may have thoughts such as: "I can't do this," "This is driving me crazy," or "I can't think."

It's in these moments that you should take three deep breaths. Taking these breaths will help you gain a sense of relief by immediately decreasing your anxious thoughts and feelings.

These three deep breaths are what I call "Harmonic Breathing". They will enliven you, invigorate you, and help you to relax. These breaths also help to decrease fatigue, enable you to focus better, and can decrease tension and pain.

Many of us just don't feel as well as we can because we don't breathe deeply enough to give us a wonderful full shot of oxygen that will improve how we feel immediately and return harmony to our body. Many times we have been breathing so shallowly that we have starved our bodies for the oxygen it needs without really being aware of it. This chronic shallow breathing throws off the balance of oxygen and carbon dioxide causing fatigue, inability to focus, anxiety, moodiness, and other concerns.

This may just be a habit we have developed or we may actually be responding to the stressors of life, like the noise of city living—sirens, jack hammers, people in rush hour traffic and yet our bodies trying to cope with these irritants chronically sits in the "fight or flight" response pattern. We hold our breath, we tighten our belly, we tighten our shoulders carrying the burdens and stressors of our world creating a chronic stress reaction with adrenal glands on our kidneys pumping out cortisol to increase our physical alertness in this "fight or flight" pattern. Our breathing increases to quick shallow breaths and our heart rate increases. Now this was fine and effective and even essential in the Stone Age when saber tooth tigers were chasing us, but now the chronic stress and "fight or flight" response causes us all sorts of aggravation and concern.

The "Harmonic Breathing" can change this stress chemistry very quickly.

Of course this type of breathing is akin to many of the ancient practices that have taught breathing techniques for thousands of years in yoga, Buddhist breath meditations, and Christian contemplative practices.

When you breathe in, relax your lower abdominal muscles and allow the abdomen to expand. As you do so just lift your chin slightly and tilt your head up slightly as well. Consciously relax and release your neck and shoulder muscles expanding and stretching your spine upward as if you are sitting up taller. Roll slightly forward as you breathe in and feel the diaphragm expand as you deeply inhale. When you are at the maximum of your inhale pause briefly and then exhale.

When you breathe out, bring your chin down, your head forward, roll your spine forward, contract your abdominal muscles and feel your diaphragm shorten and the air push out of your lungs. Then pause for a few seconds until your body says, "okay it's time to breathe in"—you will know when this point is reached and then inhale again.

Do this three times in a row to decrease the stress response and feel the relaxation begin, focus return, fatigue ease, and anxiety release.

While you take the breaths, stay present in the moment that is NOW.

Anchor yourself to that moment. Be fully present in the moment and just breathe in the relaxed state.

Truly, there is nothing more important than taking three deep breaths to regain the feeling of harmony within.

To increase the likelihood that you will use the three breathes strategy it is a good idea to send out the APB throughout your day. You do this by using awareness cues.

Awareness cues help you create a new habit by linking it with an everyday activity you are currently doing.

For example, before getting out of bed in the morning, before you even open your eyes, take three deep breaths. Link it to your morning coffee—take three deep breaths before you take your first sip. Associate the APB with answering the phone—pause for a moment—take three deep breaths before answering the phone—I found phone conversations quite difficult so it was a perfect time for me to use the three harmonizing breaths of the APB.

MESSAGE 2

*Malachi has taught me to be aware
of my non-verbal messages.*

*H*orses of course, rarely speak, or at least the majority of people don't hear what they are saying but we can see what they are saying. When I bring people to the horses I always tell them about the horse's ears. This is one observable way that they are telling you if they are ok in the moment with you —the ears are straight up, this is an indication that all is well. If the ears are half way back, look around, it is either you are starting to invade the horse's space too quickly or another horse is around that they are telling clearly to take caution. Last, if you see the ears lying flat back against the head—BACK OFF! Regain your awareness and attention to what you are doing and give the horse a wee bit of space. The tail, the eyes, and the hooves will all tell you very clearly what the horse is telling you about how he is feeling.

We do this as well. The way we express ourselves is through our movements but often we do it unconsciously and portray a message that perhaps we didn't mean to. Crossing your arms when talking to someone indicates you may not be receptive to what the person is saying. Not making eye contact may imply you are distracted or not listening.

Answering or texting on your phone while conversing with someone is not only rude, but clearly indicates that the person on the other end of that phone is more important than I am standing in front of you.

Our technology allows us to be constantly connected with each other, and indeed, the whole world. I can phone, text, email, or Skype with someone in Scotland easily and quickly. There are few places, unless you consciously choose to turn off your cell phone, that you cannot be reached. I used to text and ride the horse or catch a call regarding work while out riding. This is definitely looking for an accident to happen and so we must be conscious of what we are doing when we send or receive calls and text messages.

I have always emphasized with my girls that if you have a problem with someone you need to see them. Texting just doesn't get the message through correctly as it would if you stood in front of the person. Sending a text doesn't offer the intonation in your voice, or extend the feelings of care, concern, and compassion that being in front of the person can indicate which will help to diffuse a misunderstanding. We have tried to correct this by adding "emotions" to our texts. A smiling cartoon face, a "lol" to indicate we are kidding or just having fun, or a frown to say we are sorry, sad, or just feel bad for the person. But it cannot, nor ever will replace the face-to-face connection, communication, and care of real personal contact.

Why is this? Gregg Braden in *The Spontaneous Healing of Belief* writes that there is an energy field that surrounds every cell and your very being and this invisible field is influenced by your beliefs. It is actually the sole governing entity that influences the body. He believes, "we are bathed in a field of intelligent energy that fills what used to be thought of as empty space. Additional discoveries show beyond any reasonable doubt that this field responds to us. It rearranges itself in the presence of our heart-based feelings and beliefs."[7] Remember the energy round pen

7 Dyer, Wayne, *Excuses Be Gone*, Hay House, *USA, 2010. Pg. 26.*

experience I had with the horse? It was this heart-felt connection that communicated my emotional state. Input from the heart facilitates the experience of positive feeling states, heightened mental clarity, improved decision-making, and increased creativity. In the presence of another, the heart secretes oxytocin, which is often referred to as the bonding or love hormone for cognition, tolerance, adaptation, and caring behaviours. We know intuitively that it is the heart that reveals our authentic true self rather than just the mind's opinion, preferences, and habits.

There is a radiating force or electromagnetic field that emerges out of our heart and surrounds the body spiraling from the heart called a torus. It "embraces" our body with the "same makeup as our planetary torus-forms arising from the earth as the earth's magnetic fields stream out into space so does the hearts electromagnetic fields from our body"[8] It is a triple torus, three fold surrounding our bodies. The innermost "energy field" registers our physical sensations, the middle torus is our emotional or relational connection and influences, and our third torus expands into the spiritual domain.

As we connect to another our energies connect and radiate our innermost feelings and deepest thoughts. The horse with its large heart and gut can sense and feel what we are experiencing within and mirror this in a round pen interaction. We affect through our silent beliefs and thoughts what we want others to believe and see within us.

Strategy for non-verbal body language awareness

We can observe our physical reactions to gain self-awareness. We do this to help participants in our horse programs to become more aware of the layers of connectivity. Ask a friend, your partner, or co-worker to stand approximately ten feet away from you. Now begin to approach this person and watch for indications that you have entered into a layer of connection with them. How will you know? The person may blink,

8   Pearce Chilton Joseph, *The Heart-Miind Matrix*, 2012. Pg. 71

tighten her lips, lean backwards, or smile, and even laugh. When you notice this, rather than continuing to approach, move back to the foot that has not advanced closer and just take a deep breath and release it with an audible sigh. Relax and see the change in the person you are advancing towards.

Try this again but rather than stopping when you see an indication of the layer of connection keep advancing and watch the person's response to this. You may see her body become tense, her breathing may shorten, or she may even laugh to express her discomfort. We do this all too often with people. Rather than allowing them the space they need to feel comfortable we rush in and start talking, or shoving files at them, or assigning work that needs to be done. Now I am not suggesting that at work you start "rolling back" as you approach your co-workers as this could trigger some serious reservations about your sanity. However, we can notice the reaction in others and take a deep breath to relax, which will help the other person as well. We all have this capability to observe, respond, and allow others the space they need to be comfortable. This will allow greater clarity of expression and more effective cooperation.

With another person present you can also recall a time that you became angry and get that person's feedback. Does your jaw clench, your lips press tight together, your eyes narrow, and/or your shoulders tense? Perhaps your breathing becomes shallow and your hands are now tightened in a fist. Rather than continuing in this rigid stance take a deep breath two or three times and as you do consciously think about allowing your jaw to relax and your shoulders to drop. Change how you react to this memory in your physical body. You can consciously harness your attention and how you are reacting, pause, and breathe.

Try doing this again with your partner but think of a wonderful memory. Think of a time that you had fun and were excited about an activity. Let your partner express what she sees in your expression—your body and what she feels you are experiencing. Now return to the memory of anger and consciously choose to relax as you are in this favorable memory. If we are open to change and we don't cling to our patterns of behavior or to ideas of how events "should" be rather how they "are", we can consciously choose to react differently. It is the pause in the APB that we talked about that will give you the opportunity to react differently. Just pause and breathe to observe yourself without any preconceived ideas of how the scene that is unfolding before you should go. You can objectively select a different reaction to allow opportunity, connection, and choice to enter in.

We cannot always choose what events unfold before us but we can choose how we react. We always have this ability even though you may not like all of the choices. Anger and frustration are automatic reactions that arise because we are attached to our ideas of how things should unfold.

"It is as it is." Events may be neither good nor bad, they just are, it is how we interpret and respond that gives it meaning. There are horrendous circumstances that we as humans can impose upon others. I am not trying to downplay that in the least, yet we cannot change the past. We can only change ourselves. Forgiveness, releasing what "should have been", and the anger we may feel for what has occurred is a gift that is truly available to you. Your replaying an interaction with another in your head again and again and wishing it had gone differently only aggravates and I believe, develops into health issues that express a desire of the soul to release and let go to find peace, hope, and love. Many physical illnesses can be linked to stress, anxiety, and difficulty coping with "what is". Hey it isn't easy, I get that, but for your own physical well-being, for the relationship you are losing, for the love that is being restrained, I would ask that you try the exercises above and gain insight and awareness of what may be expressed through your non-verbal cues.

MESSAGE 3

*Malachi has taught me to listen to
what my body is saying to me*

"Hearty laughter is a good way to jog internally without having to
go outdoors."

—Norman Cousins

Our bodies tell us much more than we realize and help us to
deal directly with emotions and feelings that may be bottled
up within us. Connection, expression, and release are essential
to experience true joy and renewed health. Horses and animals in the
wild respond to what is needed in the moment. They eat when they are
hungry, they rest when it is needed, and they play when joy erupts.

There is nothing wrong with taking a break or even taking a nap.
Our daily schedules may not include time for a wee nap but rather
than going to grab more coffee and partake in the drama that may be
unfolding in the lunchroom you can choose to go outside or to a quiet
spot where you can engage in the APB. You can take the time to reflect

and ask yourself, "How is my day going?" "Why am I feeling a particular way?" "What should I do differently to help myself cope with what is happening around me?" Or just allow the silence to expand within. There may not be true silence, but the silence I am speaking of is that which you can create within. With practice by frequently initiating the APB and breathing deeply, releasing thoughts and tension for three deep breaths, the easier this will become and the less you will be distracted. Peace is really an inside job. It can only begin with you.

I used to have tightness and pain in my right trapezes muscle, until Thor, the Percheron horse at Wendy and Andre's helped me to understand that I was carrying all of my frustrations there. I came to understand that frustration, in this area, indicated that something had to change in my life. Part of the frustration and tension I was experiencing was a result of my endless desire to return to the person I was pre-fall. Again this was all an "inside job". No one else was trying to make me return to who I was and likely my family appreciated the person I had become. Yet I felt this person who tired easily, was overly sensitive, unable to multitask, and make decisions was of little worth in a society of action, production, and speed.

As I have stated numerous times, awareness is the key to finding peace, joy, and hope in life. I needed to be aware that this was what was causing a physical reaction within my body, how my negative condemning thoughts were adversely affecting me and to choose to think, act, and react differently. It was the horses that helped me to process this in their mirroring of my anxiety and frustration, in their intuitive touch, and abiding presence. When I could quiet my physical being—heart, mind, and soul, I could connect within to truly know what they were trying to express to me in their actions in a round pen.

Our bodies really do tell us what they need and it will get your attention one way or another whether it is getting a virus and contracting a cold, or by tension and pain in your neck and back, or by tiring you so greatly that you must lie down. We try to push on past the pain, through the cold, or ignore the exhaustion but if ignored, greater damage can occur. I suffer from migraine headaches when I become stressed and overwhelmed. I had a migraine that lasted nine days with full photosensitivity, nausea, excruciating pain, and the need to stay in a darkened, quiet, bedroom. I have even had left-side paralysis that sometimes accompanies these symptoms. We need to listen to our bodies and ask it what it needs. Perhaps if I rested or if I expressed what I needed to my family, friends, or associates I could avoid these headaches. The following strategies will help you to gain awareness of the messages that your body may be giving you and also a few tips to help you to relax and find a wee bit of peace from within.

Strategy for Body and Sensation Awareness
Progressive body relaxation sessions can enable you to feel what it is like to relax, flow, and be present to the moment. (To experience this please go to my website at www.creatingharmonywithin.com.) You will be able to consciously and purposefully choose this feeling rather than tension and the habitual stress reactions that you have become accustomed to. As part of your relaxation sessions, do not just start the progressive relaxation but do a quick scan from head to toe and connect to what you are feeling in your body before you start to initiate the relaxation response to your conscious connection within.

Start at the top of your head as I did during the reflective round pen experience with the horses. Think of it as a beam of light or scan that is going from the top of your head to the tips of your toes and connect and become aware of any tingling, pain, heat, coolness, or tension you may feel and even what comes into your mind. Perhaps a color will be associated with a particular area or a word may pop into your head. Be aware of the sensation then continue to flow through the scan to see if there is any other area that may need your attention. Once you have done this and you are aware of an area that has "spoken" to you, breathe into it. Take a deep breath with your mind focused on the area that you felt a sensation in and see if there is anything that comes into your mind about that sense of awareness that you have now brought your body to. How long has there been pain in this area? How often does this area feel tight? Was there heat or cold or a tingling there and how often has this occurred and you have ignored it?

The horses help us to reconnect to this in an innate, intuitive way. I once had a client who had experienced extreme trauma and had been to traditional talk therapy and her social worker felt that she would benefit from the experience with the horses. Her first experience with Malachi helped her to reconnect to that which had been causing her such agony and fear to release it by literally lying over Malachi's side and back. Although I couldn't tell you logically at the time why I was asking her to do this, I instructed her to lean over Malachi and into him and put her right hand on his withers and her left hand on his croup area.

The withers are just at the end of the mane where it rises to the horse's back and the croup is just above the tail on the back. I taught kids at camp to remember not to get behind the croup by reminding them that this is where the horse would poop and kick and certainly no one wanted that but from the side where I had her asked her to stand was safe. The withers jut out slightly and so she was able to put her hand there, which was above the heart chakra and the croup was just above the sacral chakra, which are powerful energetic connections.

Not only was she connected by her hands, she also pressed her body into his side which connected heart to heart and engaged the parasympathetic nervous system, that which is the calming by vagus nerve stimulation. The vagus nerve is the 10th cranial nerve that has extensive motor and sensory fibers that pass through the neck and thorax to the abdomen. It wraps your heart and is considered the seat of intuition and compassion.

The autonomic nervous system has two components that balance each other—the sympathetic nervous system (SNS) is for protection and initiates the fight or flight response and the parasympathetic nervous system (PNS) helps to relax and calm you. The SNS responds in times of stress and the PNS helps you to de-stress and decrease the stress response. Thus the sympathetic and parasympathetic nervous systems work together to help alert you to danger and return your body to relaxation. If you are constantly in stress mode, or your fears and worries never allow for relaxation, you may experience negative effects such as depression, anxiety, insomnia, and difficulty thinking and maintaining attention because of overstimulation of the SNS and an imbalance in cortisol that is secreted at times of stress.

To engage the vagus nerve, which connects to the PNS, I asked her to lean over the horse and take deep breathes to relax and expand her diaphragm. By stimulating the vagus nerve it would decrease the stress response and help her to relax and block the hormone cortisol, which is running amuck due to the constant stress she had been experiencing. It also decreases the chance of a stress headache and helps to overcome depression and anxiety, as well as, enabling a person to sleep better.

I did this with a horse at Wendy's and had an incredible journey of being one with the universe and feeling all of the heartbeats around the world. I know it is unbelievable but in that moment I sensed the heartbeat of babies as they were being born, beating in rhythm, and all beings upon the earth. In that moment I sensed and felt the entire rhythm of the earth and our connection. It was a lovely gift from Redman. It was also a wee bit overwhelming for me to sense this especially with my new emotional sensitivity from the accident. I give thanks that Wendy and Andre were there at the time and that I knew some strategies which I am referring to below that help to calm, rebalance, and regain focus.

If you don't have a horse to lean over, you can activate the vagus nerve by breathing slowly and deeply as I instructed in the expansion of the APB. We usually breathe about 14 breaths per minute. If you could slow this to seven times per minute by counting as was instructed earlier, it will help to oxygenate the body's cells and produce endorphins which are the body's "feel good" hormones. So breathe, breathe, breathe—deep and long and feel your chest and diaphragm expand. Do not rush it. Just take your mind out and breathe.

"OHM" chanting or "Toning" can also stimulate the vagus nerve and help the stress response. Hold the "O" part of the Ohm for at least four seconds then proceed to the "M" for eight seconds. Don Campbell, who is the founder of the Institute of Music, Health, and Education states that "Nothing rivals toning." Toning is making sounds with elongated vowels like OHM or sounds like Ahhhhhhhhh, which help you to become more centered in your body, enhance your ability to relax, decrease anxiety, fear, and other emotions, and reduce physical pain. Dr. Amen tells us in *Change Your Brain Change Your Life*[9] that toning balances brain waves, deepens the breath, reduces the heart rate, and imparts a general sense of wellbeing.

As you are doing this breathing and the OM sounds try to clear the mind again, allow the body to relax, and to embody this further touch your thumb to each finger on your hand to count out the seconds.

Another way to get the PNS to relax is by **touching your lips**. Well I guess that tells us why kissing is so relaxing! I have an unconscious habit of playing with my lips while I watch television or if I am reading. Funny enough so do my three older sisters. It is a habit that we have somehow picked up and now my daughter Megan does it as well. Unconsciously we must have known of the calming and relaxing power of the PSN as we did this.

Thymus thumps are another great way to decrease stress and also help your immune system, help to get your energy flowing, and improve oxygen flow. And this relief doesn't just happen at the time you do the

---

9   Amen, Dr., *Change Your Brain Change Your Life,*

Three Thymus Thumps—there will be a cumulative effect over time that helps you to feel more focused, energized, and optimistic. Thymus comes from the Greek word thymos, which actually means "life energy." This flow of energy throughout your body may be blocked due to the stress that you are experiencing in your life. The thymus is a link between the mind and body—and due to stress—it may shrink which will make you feel less energized. You can rebalance this life energy within you by simply thumping the thymus gland. To do the thymus thump just tap in the middle of the sternum about an inch below where a man's tie would be. Place your index and second finger in the U notch at the top of the breastbone and slide them down about an inch and tap three times. Do this to the beat of a waltz—one-two-three—over and over again.

You can do this before jumping out of bed to help increase energy and wellbeing or anytime during the day. But don't do this before going to bed as it may energize and awaken you when you want to shut down and rest. It doesn't have to attract attention—just tap three times gently and no one will even notice!

Smile. Yes, a smile. It will make a huge difference in the way that you feel and how you relate to others. A smile will help you relax, feel less stress, and help you feel more confident when you are overwhelmed or over stimulated. When we smile our bodies release endorphins that improve the way we are feeling and help us to naturally relax. A smile is viewed across cultures as a sign of friendliness, connection, and understanding. When you smile others respond positively to you— smiling is contagious—it is a universal sign of happiness. So turn that frown upside down and smile (even if it feels corny) because it takes less work to smile than it does to frown.

Laughter is good for the soul. It boosts your immune system, helps fight infections, lifts depression, fights disease, decreases blood pressure, decreases stress hormones, increase endorphins, and will give you an improved sense of well-being. Children laugh over 300 times a day but adults usually about 15 times a day. Children laugh unconditionally and it isn't dependent on the laughter of others so perhaps this is why Jesus used them as a reference to the kingdom and sense of heaven. Norman Cousins, who is thought to be the father of "laughter therapy", healed himself of a life threatening form of arthritis through his own self-treatment of laughter. He was given very little chance of recovering and when traditional therapies were not helping, Norman checked himself out of the hospital and into a hotel where he took mega doses of Vitamin C and watched funny movies. This allowed him to sleep pain free and eventually he became well again. So rent a great movie or watch a great TV sitcom like "I Love Lucy" if you can find them or just play a game with a child and laugh to experience unrestricted joy.

Yawn. Yes, yawn! Yawn, even when you don't feel like it. Yawning stimulates the brain's precuneus giving you increased focus and also helps you to relax. It also cools off the brain, relieves drowsiness, helps you communicate, and increases your feeling of compassion and connectedness to others because when you yawn, others will start to yawn as well! Fake yawn until you can get a good long true one out. Do this eight to ten times whether you feel the need to yawn or not—it only takes 30 seconds and can truly help you feel much better!

MESSAGE 4

Malachi told me to release the "itty bitty shitty committee" and embrace the herd as my community

How did I come to this realization? Perhaps you, like my husband, ask "Who told you that?" Honestly, I believe it was Malachi that told me, to which my husband responded, "What? Malachi?"

I did an activity that we call overcoming obstacles with my horses Malachi and Bill. To do this you sit and write out what you feel is blocking you from feeling fulfilled or successful. Virginia and I did this one morning when she visited and I wrote the two obstacles that I felt were constricting me. The first was the good opinion of others and the second was financial worries.

Once you have written your blocks, you go to the horses and seek one to help you overcome what you have identified as barriers. When I arrived at the fence Bill was there. This was odd as Bill and Brad were rarely apart, yet he was right at the gate as I approached. I put the halter around him and opened the gate to allow him to follow me to the dome. Malachi was a few feet away but he approached so quickly that he came through the gate with Bill. What could I do but ask Virginia to grab another halter?

Now this isn't the first time that horses have come through the gate unexpectedly. We were awakened one morning at about 6 a.m. by two police officers asking us if we had horses. "Um—yes." "Are they all accounted for?" "I think so"—but nope all ten were gone. I had been out riding and had left the gate at the end of the corral open so they must have exited sometime during the night. There was a report that they had been seen near a major roadway in our area. So off the police go with Doug and me in tow—on the "Gator" and the other ATV. I unfortunately got turned in the wrong direction and by the time I turned back the horses were found in a field grazing.

I was relieved to see them all and parked the gator across the road to head to the other side to check that all was well. As I crossed the road all of the horses raised their head and it seemed that they all moved in unison towards me. It felt very powerful. The police officer said to me, "Well we know who feeds them." Yet I don't feed them in the way that he was thinking for their physical wellbeing. But I do feed them energetically engaging in a heart connection of unconditional love, authenticity, and mutual respect. The time I spend just hanging out with them, the love I feel and the energetic unconditional connection and being open to the moment is what is important.

We began to put halters on them, which was uneventful although the police felt they would run from the "handcuffs". We didn't have a trailer to take them back so I took three, Doug took three, a neighbor took two and a police officer took two and off down the road we walked with the police lights flashing to escort them back to the paddock.

On this day however, I was able to put halters on both Bill and Malachi and direct them to the dome where I would "overcome" the obstacles that had become lodged in my subconscious as paradigms or agreements I had made with my "tribe", family, or community. I chose two items to represent the blocks in my life—a railroad tie for money and a mat for community.

I kept Bill on the lead but took Malachi's off and he followed right along beside Bill. It was wonderful to have him beside me by choice and not by the "suggestion" of the lead rope. I approached the first obstacle—money. There seemed to be no hesitation—across this we went. There is abundance everywhere they conveyed. The only lack is in your mind. Nature and all of creation reveal that abundance and prosperity is yours to claim and to help others actualize. I would later delve deeper into this and realize that I felt unworthy and undeserving. I had always been given all that I needed and more from my parents. Yet when my father died, I remember saying, "I hope I am worthy." This began a small thought that perhaps I wasn't. Perhaps I wouldn't be a good steward. I listened to others who were struggling and trying to hold on tightly to what they claimed, but lost, and this soon became my paradigm as well. When offered money I would crumple it quickly and shove it into my pocket as if I didn't deserve it or that it was unacceptable. This activity helped me to realize that I am deserving and worthy, and that I am a good steward.

The next was the rubber mat and the "good opinion of others." How funny that I should choose a mat that was "walked on" often. If we allow the good opinion of others to affect us we will always have a roller coaster ride of emotion. If someone compliments you, you will feel up and if not you will feel down. Approval, prestige, compliments, getting to the top, getting your name recognized, awards, and power are dangerous drugs that we are given to reward societal approval and norms. Yet it is a game that we will never win.

As we approached the mat representing my need for "the good opinion of others" I felt a hesitation in my step. Malachi however did not hesitate. He stepped over the mat, Bill and I followed and I know he clearly shared with me "We are your community now." I was not to feel overwhelmed or rejected by the community that surrounded our farm, and in reality, there was no purposeful exclusion by my community. It was only my preconceived paradigms, false beliefs, and ego that instilled these thoughts in my mind. Now I felt affirmed, welcomed, and authentic in the presence of the horses as they would assist me to build my confidence and ability to once again return to the community beyond my home by their acceptance and love of who I had become.

Strategies to fire the "Itty Bitty Shitty Committee"

Keeping your thoughts, words, and deeds positive, hope filled, and affirming is important to building confidence and authentic being into your life. With positive statements and confidence we can fire the "Itty Bitty Shitty Committee." Here are a few strategies to help you create that in your life.

Affirmations are positive statements that you write and read again and again in your car, while making coffee, while in the shower, or cutting grass. Affirmations can be repeated silently in your head when you feel down or challenged or out loud—preferably in appropriate situations not when standing in line to grab a coffee! By doing this you can change the paradigms or unconscious beliefs that are creating negative reactions and feelings.

Basically every thought you think is self-talk, inner dialogue, and a flow of affirmations. We are constantly affirming subconsciously with our words and thoughts to create our life experience in every moment. It is a reflection of your inner truth and beliefs that are embedded in your subconscious. Affirmations can be either positive or negative and we use the behaviour patterns we have automatically learned to respond and react to many of our everyday events.

By using positive affirming statements you are changing your neural connections within the reticular activating system (RAS) and these learned behaviour patterns and responses. The RAS plays an important role in the function of the body such as breathing, sleeping, and heartbeat. The most important part of the RAS is to maintain consciousness and so while asleep it reduces its work and while awake it increases.

The RAS senses things around us and helps us to sort them out. Every function you do is either consciously or unconsciously initiated. The RAS is responsible for several functions that are related to your awareness and consciousness. It is like a gateway between your conscious and subconscious minds. It takes messages from the conscious mind and embeds them into your subconscious mind at your request. If something good occurs it is treated as positive and similarly if you are thinking something negative, the RAS help you to realize the presence of a negative impact. The RAS can choose to make a problem larger or smaller. If we focus on something that seems positive then positive feelings and reactions will emote. But be warned that if you constantly focus upon the negative these things may eventually end up causing a negative impact in your life.

Through the RAS you are put in the driver's seat in charge of your emotions, your thoughts, your motivations, your focus, and your actions. It filters out the deluge of irrelevant information based on what is of current interest to your mind (a huge job) and tries to allow only important details through to be processed. "Where focus goes, attention flows." But remember, focus on what you want, not what you do not want. Do not focus on what you do not have or what is negative in your life as that will be what is attracted to you. It may not really be what you want, but if you keep your focus on this it is what will be delivered to you. Stephen Covey has summed up the RAS perfectly, "We see the world as we are, not as it is."

By continually repeating an affirmation with hope, enthusiasm, and excitement even the strongest convictions can be changed. You would be hard pressed to find any self-help program that did not use affirmations as they are so important to change negative beliefs and paradigms and helping you to initiate new behaviours. As you consciously choose to repeat positive statements it will become easier and natural to think of the good, the better, and the best, which will be reflected in your outer experience.

When writing your affirmations use only positive emotion packed words with lots of descriptive adjectives and focus on what you do want not what you don't want. "I" and "AM" are the two strongest words to assist us in achieving our dreams. The "I Am" is the deepest part of you and so start your affirmations with it:

I AM happy and at peace.

I AM my perfect weight.

I AM loving and deserve love.

I AM the woman who is so happy and grateful.

Being grateful now acknowledges even the smallest of blessings to show you are already happy and grateful for what is now. It is acknowledging that you are already the things that you are affirming in your life!

I AM so happy and grateful that I have great health NOW.

I AM so happy and grateful that I have a wonderful job.

I AM so happy and grateful that wonderful things flow easily into my life.

Affirmations are more than just repeating the words however. It is important to engage positive emotions such as joy, excitement, passion, and hope. Positive emotions help to increase the vibration of your attraction to like circumstances. And here are other ways to help you in your affirmations:

Write out your affirmations again and again to help you imprint it on your mind. Write it out at least ten times and then say it out loud with passion and excitement.

Say it in front of a mirror! One of the most effective ways is to say our affirmations in front of a mirror. Look at yourself straight in the eye and repeat your affirmations with a smile and a pump of your arm with a big "woot woot" at the end. Sure it looks silly! But get that enthusiasm in there and you will magnify the importance of the message to yourself.

Sing your affirmation. They are much more effective when you sing them to imprint them into your mind. Add movement with the song and you secure it even deeper in the subconscious.

Leave notes and cards sitting around so you see them often throughout the day.

Affirmations can help you to achieve your goals and dreams when you concentrate positively on achieving them. How does this work? First you have to be very clear what you want and be excited, joyful, and pumped up about it. As I have stated again and again it is very important to ensure that you feel the positive emotions.

Second, once you have found your dream goal you must take persistent actions to send the message of your goal to the subconscious brain over and over again through activities such as visualizing how your life would be once you have achieved this goal, writing and reading your goal again and again and again, and connecting your goal to an emotional feeling or event. The RAS enhances the positive, the powerful, and the ability to change and experience happiness, success, joy, love, and other wonderful feelings by consciously choosing them. It is the gatekeeper to awareness, motivation, and your focus towards important goals in your life. It directs what your brain focuses on and finds more of that for you.

It is important to always return your focus to the positive, the good, and to use the affirmations to direct yourself towards the things you truly desire. Know what you want and direct it there! It requires practice and repetition to make a habit and takes approximately 45 days of repetition to change a habit. What you practice again and again will create a stronger relationship. The great news is that when you choose to focus on the positive and that which you truly desire, it will become stronger and stronger and the neural nets for the negative become weaker and weaker until they no longer have an effect on you. You need to do that and do it consistently and frequently.

To obtain positive outcomes:

1. Use a journal to write your goal as clearly as you can.
2. Write it in the past tense as though you have already achieved it.
3. Always include positive emotions such as gratitude, contentment, joy, happiness, simplicity, love, and so on.
4. State your goal with I AM. They are the two strongest and magnetic words in the world. It is the "I AM" that can empower you to joy and love for it is that which is your soul and will enliven your "soul" purpose.
5. Write your dream goal out again and again and again.
6. Record it and listen to it to imprint it upon your subconscious mind.
7. Close your eyes and envision what it will look like, feel like, and be like when you experience it.
8. Make a vision board of photos of you smiling, enjoying life, and surrounded by the family, friends, and environment you love.
9. Post notes on your fridge, mirror, car dashboard, door frame, cupboards, TV—everywhere and anywhere with positive statements, affirmations, and feelings that align you with what you desire.
10. Please do not focus on what is missing or use negative words. Keep it pure and positive.

11. Always focus on love. If someone is irritating me, is talking negative, or I find myself passing judgment I repeat the word, "Love, love, love" and this helps to change my attitude. If you are critical—criticism will return to you. If you are angry—anger will be returned to you. If you speak of lack—lack will be sure to follow you. What goes around truly comes around! What you sow you also reap. Wish only the best for others!

12. Be the best you can be by focusing on your best beliefs, emotions, sensations, and thoughts and that will come back to you.

Gratefulness! Being grateful is one of the most important, empowering, and positive things you can do for yourself. Practice it daily! Journal daily what you are grateful for that has created joy, love, prosperity, and great health in your life. Find even the smallest thing to be grateful for and this too shall be drawn to you. As you journal positive, loving, grateful thoughts you will recognize more and more that you can be grateful for.

By keeping a **Gratitude Journal** you will see patterns that are occurring in your life. You may see negative patterns that you can change. It helps you to see that there is always something to be grateful for even in the ordinary times of your life.

1. So grab your goal and affirmation journal or a second journal if you want to keep a separate one that you can use daily to write in.

2. Write in your favorite inspirational quotes that will lift you each time you refer back to them.

3. Do this at the start of your day to give it a boost straight away. Even before you open your eyes ask yourself (or the person beside you!) "What am I grateful for today?" Then

write down whatever comes into your mind that you can be grateful for today.

4. Try to find three things you are grateful for, or just one if that is all that comes to you. But as you do this again and again more and more will come to you that you will appreciate and be grateful for. Done in conjunction with the positive affirmations you are embedding within the subconscious through the RAS you will experience the positive and be hope filled.

5. Read your gratitude journal every day and all of the reasons that you are thankful.

You may be wondering how long it takes to see the positive changes in your life that you are affirming. It really is about consistency and believability. Ask yourself these questions to see if you truly are in alignment with your dreams and positivity.

Do you truly believe and affirm what you are saying?

Can you see the new and powerful hope filled life you are claiming?

Do you sense any resistance in your body, emotions, or conflicting negative thoughts when you are doing this?

If you do feel any resistance breathe, breathe, breathe, and return to your affirmations.

Focus on what you have done well and what you are committed to and ask yourself—

What did I do well today?

What positive steps did I make towards changing my thoughts, feelings, and emotions to better ones?

What did I do today for another?

If a negative thought occurs forgive yourself, forget it, and move on. Dwelling on an angry outburst or negative thinking will only create negative experiences and embed them within the RAS and enhance the negative. So let it go and regain focus and have fun, enjoyment, and allow ease and joy to return. This should be fun! A life of ease and flow, knowing that good things always return to you will make your days light and filled with the outlook that will naturally begin to see the positive.

Random acts of kindness—On occasion in the drive through line to get my coffee I will pay for the coffee of the person in the car behind me. I think of the joy and the positive lift that the person behind me will feel and hope that she does that or something even better for someone because she experienced an unexpected treat and act of kindness. Yes, what you sow you will reap so wish for others at all times that which you wish for yourself.

MESSAGE 5

Malachi taught me to watch and harness what I think if it is positive, uplifting, and hope-filled because others truly can hear your silent thoughts. These thoughts come out in your actions and will determine your destiny, relationships, and satisfaction in life.

"Be careful what you think, for your thoughts become your words. Be careful what you say, for your words become your actions. Be careful what you do, for your actions become your habits. Be careful what becomes habitual, for your habits become your destiny."

—Author Unknown

"Finally, brothers and sisters, whatever is true, whatever is noble, whatever is right, whatever is pure, whatever is lovely, whatever is

*admirable—if anything is excellent or praiseworthy—think about
such thing"* (Phillippians 4:8).[10]

Two great sayings that harness the importance of what we think
about. As humans we have 40–50,000 random thoughts in a day. We
think, imagine, and ponder all sorts of things that we don't even realize
we are registering in our minds. We create all sorts of stories about what
happened or what might happen rather than just focusing on the NOW.

Why so negative Eeyore?

Dr. Rick Hanson states in the book *Buddha's Brain* that "our
brain typically detects negative information faster than positive
information."

When you experience a negative event your hippocampus
makes sure it is stored for future reference.

The saying "Once burned, twice shy" comes into effect. "Your
brain is like Velcro for negative experiences and Teflon for positive
ones—even though most of your experiences are probably neutral
or positive."

It really is in our nature to think negatively so it is essential that you
consciously implant positive thoughts throughout your day. Your brain
has a built-in "negativity bias" (Vaish, Grossman, and Woodward 2008)
that primes you for avoidance.

---

10 The Holy Bible, The New Revised Standard Version, Oxford Press, Anglicized
    Edition, Oxford University Press 1998. Philippians 4:8

"The negativity bias fosters or intensifies other unpleasant emotions, such as anger, sorrow, depression, guilt, and shame. It highlights past losses and failures, it downplays present abilities, and it exaggerates future obstacles. Consequently, the mind continually tends to render unfair verdicts about a person's character, conduct, and possibilities. The weight of those judgments can really wear you down."[11]

How Negative Biases Intensify?

Let's say that you are at a stop light in a busy intersection. The light turns green but you have lost awareness of all that is going on around you in a moment of daydreaming.

The car behind you honks, and you are startled into awareness. Your sympathetic nervous system lights up like a Christmas tree releasing epinephrine! Your heart is racing, you grip the steering wheel, your muscles tense, your pupils dilate, you are breathing shallow, and you are ready to take action.

The occipital area of the brain sends a message in two different directions. One to the hippocampus that refers to similar experiences from your past and alerts the amygdala, which quickly evaluates the threat. It initiates the "fight or flight" neural and hormonal systems.

Now in the world of saber tooth tigers this "fight or flight" was essential. You would see a saber tooth tiger—the hippocampus would quickly check for similar experiences from the past then screams "Run!" and quickly the alarm rings throughout your entire body. Yet in a world where there are constant stressors, ambulance and police sirens, honking cars, anxiety because of all your "to dos",

---

11   Hanson, Rick & Siegel Dan, *Buddha's Brain*, New Harbinger Publications, 2009. Pg. 42.

the fear of being late to work raise our bodies to high alert level of stress frequently throughout our day. The long term effect of this can have detrimental effects on our health and well-being as we will see below.

The implicit memory has now initiated the amygdala, which has formed implicit memories from previous experiences, and refers to these experiences, evaluates and initiates the question of "fight or flight"—to run or not to run These are memories of past experiences that reside just below the conscious level in the subconscious.

The amygdala continually incites fear and anxiety from the implicit memory that it has stored regardless of the current situation you are facing and of the intensity of the situation.

This chronic agitation can wear down the hippocampus due to the frequent initiation of the "fight or flight" syndrome, which is the sympathetic nervous system. The adrenal glands release cortisol in response to the pituitary gland that activates the hypothalamus and around and around we go. It becomes a vicious circle with over secretion of cortisol and ongoing agitation, which leads to unease and distress.

How can we change this? Using the APB frequently throughout the day to check in with yourself and breathe, breathe, breathe. Do the three deep harmonic breaths and hold on your maximum exhalation until you feel you need to take a deep inhalation again. This helps to decrease the stress response. Remember to use your affirmations throughout your day as well to assist you to focus on the positive.

We become changed by what we pay attention to be it negative or positive so hold positive good thoughts and memories for 10 – 30 seconds and savor the positive feelings, emotions, and sensations of that moment.

This little formula sums it up nicely, Time + Focus + Emotion = Change.

The more frequently you can focus on the positive and the best and add feelings of joy and gratefulness the more you will experience change and decrease the stress response.

Implicit and Explicit Memory

Implicit memory develops within the first 18 months of life. It is memory that we do not have conscious awareness of. It is something that is being recalled from our past. It can manifest as a feeling in our bodies, as emotional reaction, a perceptual bias or behaviour pattern of response, which we do not realize is from the past

Explicit memory begins by our second birthday. We are conscious that we are bringing something from our past into our awareness.

As an example, implicit memory is the memory that enables us to ride a bike. Explicit memory is when we recall the day we were taught to ride.

Strategies to Change Your Thoughts to Positive Ones

The Turn Around Phrase

I learned this at one of the horse workshops I attended at Andre and Wendy's. When you are starting to feel negative, starting to think negative thoughts about yourself, about the people around you, or perhaps just being negative about how life is going—use a "turnaround" phrase.

Do the APB and Harmonic Breathing first to gain awareness. At this point use a turnaround phrase. I use a visual with this as well. For example I imagine our horse, Iceman, saying to me when I start worrying about getting up on stage, "You go girl." I see him saying this, standing tall and strong and seeing his confidence as the Alpha leader of the herd. I also add a bit of humor to it by seeing him toss his long mane and this helps me to smile and relax.

Another example of when I use the turnaround phrase is when I get my mind racing at night with negative thoughts about finances, or my abilities, or if I can really reach my dreams. In those moments I know I need to just relax and let go. So I envision Malachi saying, "Take your mind out and breathe." Then I will do the APB and Harmonic Breathing and with each breath envision him in my presence and say again and again "Take my mind out and breathe."

By using the turnaround phrase you break the pattern of negative thoughts and feelings that will only get worse and more intense if you do not intercede right away and break them up.

What about the thoughts that lurk below the surface that we are not even conscious of?

The Conscious and Unconscious thoughts

Many times we are not even conscious of what we are thinking. Our thoughts reside just below our consciousness, yet they can impact us mentally, physically, and spiritually if we do not gain awareness and acknowledge them. It is believed that unprocessed challenges, traumas, and losses in our lives can cause or be related to severe illness. Like a black hole the pain, the sorrow, and the depression, may bring on severe health challenges.

It is said that the conscious mind has approximately 5% of the thoughts and the subconscious has 95%. The mind really is trained to respond in pre-programmed ways automatically.

If you train your *conscious mind*—that part of the mind you have control over, you can direct and choose to think positive thoughts, experience excitement, have positive expectations, and choose optimism and hopefulness that will soon become your automatic choice through the subconscious mind. The unconscious/subconscious mind is creative and it attracts that which you focus upon whether that is in your direct awareness or not. Yet it is a follower of the conscious mind. The unconscious mind can only accept what the conscious mind directs to it.

What you choose to believe is what you plant within your subconscious mind and ergo that is what you will receive or create in your life. For example, I had a hard time asking for money from people coming to see the horses and the work I would do with them. I always gave extras to the visit, always 110%, yet when it came time to pay I would apologetically put the money in my pocket quickly. So my unconscious mind is saying, "She is really uncomfortable with money. Maybe we'll just give her small amounts because she really doesn't want it."

If you repeat a thought or belief in your conscious mind again and again, it will become planted into your subconscious mind and what you believe, emote, sensate, and think will come about—be it good or bad. I can guarantee that for you because it has been proven again and again that your thoughts will always bring about what you think about the most.

I believe Bob Proctor explains the characteristics of the conscious and subconscious mind in the most brilliant way with a model of the mind and body that was originated by Dr. Thurman Fleet of San

Antonio, Texas in 1934. For simplicity I have divided the subconscious and conscious thoughts like this:

Conscious Thoughts	Subconscious Thoughts
Makes decisions	Must accept what is given to it
Can choose to act	Acts in relation to what it is given
Thinks and reason	Expresses itself in feelings and actions.

Any thought that you consciously choose to impress upon the subconscious mind becomes a fixed idea which is commonly referred to as a habit or paradigm. These then continue to express themselves without any conscious effort.

I have a video that I did one day with my driving team Brad and Bill to demonstrate how the conscious and subconscious mind works.

First I invited Brad and Bill to come into the round pen without ropes or halters on. I allowed them to just freely to roam around at will. They started to get a bit excited and bite and kick each other while I was in the round pen with them. Without a word I lifted my right arm and they went to the rail of the round pen, in perfect placement together as though I had halters and ropes on them and they circled the round pen for me. I used this to show first, their bucking and jumping were the uncontrolled thoughts, but bringing awareness, taking a breath to bring them to focus helped them to settle down.

Once I have awareness or collection, I would put their harness on. This is what harnesses the left and right brain to work together. Bill represented the left-brain as he was always focused, logical, fearless, practical and the main one to pull the wagon once I hitched it up. He was more of a leader. Bradley on the other hand was the right side of the brain. The right brain I believe is in its own way more powerful than logic. It can see beyond the restraints of what is there. The right brain is creative, flowing, emotional and intuitive. Once the harness is on you have the best of both worlds. The left-brain and right-brain are connected by the harness or in the real brain, the corpus callosum.

We now have connection to our thoughts and we have brought awareness and connection to them by the application of the harness. The subconscious mind is the cart that I attach to the harness that the brain is pulling mindlessly behind it or as the unconscious thoughts. The horses barely know it is there just like the insidious unconscious paradigms that have embedded themselves into our very being. The subconscious thoughts, like the horses' cart just follows wherever we go.

Now we have the brain connected together and attached to the subconscious cart or subconscious thoughts, yet we have no control. The mind can run off with you. It can run wild with thoughts such as "How am I going to pay the mortgage?" "I'll never be able to do this." These negative thoughts can escalate to other self-deprecating and fear-inciting thoughts that can run like wild mustangs through your mind.

Now I add the reins and myself to the equation. To stop Brad and Bill from being runaway horses, I attach the reins and sit in the cart to help them. As soon as I lift the reins they know I am there; it assures them and they trust that I will do my best to keep us safe and also to have a wee bit of fun. The cart, the subconscious mind that was just being carried away by the brain with little direction now has a guide to lead it to fun, safe, and exciting times under the direction of the reins or the conscious mind. The reins and I are the conscious mind directing the brain—the two horses—and communicating the best way to go until the horses (the brain) are trained to automatically think and act in a certain way. It becomes less of a struggle to think or direct my mind to the pure, the positive, the good, the fun, and the best when I connect and harness my thoughts, initiating rather than accepting the thoughts given to me.

After training the conscious mind to think in the positive ways anything is possible. "Be you transformed by the renewing of your mind."[12] With the conscious awareness you can dream a dream that will impact your life in ways that you could never have imagined. So "Ask, and it will be given to you; search and you will find; knock and the door will be opened for you."[13]

To do this you must believe that anything is possible if you just put your mind to it. If you harness your thoughts, emotions, and beliefs and direct them, then you can gain awareness and make changes. Whatever your desire let it exude from you. Speak of your dreams and be positive and full of hope. Yet here is a word of caution—share your dreams and visions with those that you know are going to be supportive, encouraging, and excited about what you are doing. There are some who will criticize you because they are limited by their own paradigms of thinking.

Do not dwell on limiting paradigms taught to you that are paralyzing you. Believe and have faith that you can change your thoughts and change your life.

Jesus told them, "For truly I tell you if you have faith the size of a mustard seed, you will say to this mountain, 'Move from here to there', and it will move; and nothing will be impossible for you."[14]

So take hold of the reins and choose in the moment what you will think and how you will feel. Let the past be the past. Become more aware of your thoughts in the moment. Are you thinking positive, motivating, and empowering thoughts or are you being critical, complaining, or

---

12 The Holy Bible, New Revised Standard Version, Oxford Press, Anglicized Edition, Oxford University Press 1998. Romans 12:2
13 The Holy Bible, New Revised Standard Version, Oxford Press, Anglicized Edition, Oxford University Press 1998. Luke 9-10
14 Ibid Matthew 17:20

condemning of yourself and others? As Henry Ford said, "What you think you become."

"Mind-Full-Less" to Keep Positive

Our minds are always full of thoughts, subtle awareness of our environment, interpreting what is going on around us. We need to create Mind-Full-Less moments in which the mind is clear, aware, and present to the moment we are in and not straying to what we could, would, or should have done or making a judgment about what is occurring around us.

Mind-Full-Less can be intentionally created through various practices such as meditation, centering prayer, yoga, walking a labyrinth, and prayer beads. All of these can help to focus your attention and assist you to improve focus, clarity, awareness in the moment, the ability to think within your thinking, and the ability to be able to observe what is happening and remain open to it.

Remember you have the ability to choose how you think, feel, and behave in every situation. You are responsible. You are the only person who can choose how you think, feel, and believe in every situation. You are the *only* person who can truly accomplish this. If you do not choose, do not practice awareness, pause and breathe—the subconscious memory of past beliefs and choices will kick in. And if you do not like what life is serving you, then you must become aware of what you are thinking. I can guarantee you that what you are actualizing is related to your paradigms and lack of present moment awareness and the result of autopilot responses to life.

As such, the practices of awareness and being-ness of gaining the pause, can assist and empower you to be able to focus your attention, intention, and awareness in busier more distracting moments of your day. Dan Siegel in *The Pocket Guide to Interpersonal Neurobiology* writes that mindful awareness is "a form of awareness in which we are alert and open to present experience without being swept up in judgment and prior expectations."[15]

Dr. Joseph Murphy in his book *"Think Yourself to Health, Wealth & Happiness"* writes, "Periodic withdrawal during the day from sense evidence and the noise and confusion of everyday living carries with it all the benefits of sleep—that is, you become asleep to the world of the senses and alive to the wisdom and power of your subconscious mind."[16]

Numerous studies have shown that the practice of emptying the mind and staying present to the moment you are experiencing creates empathy and improves your relationships with others, as well as many health benefits. Practices that help us focus on the current moment can decrease the stress response, improve our breathing for relaxation, help increase coping and tolerance in challenging situations, reduce chronic pain, improve immune system response, and enhance our sense of wellbeing.

Remember this funny acronym—feed the *BEAR*—Breathing Engages Awareness and Response-ableness—so you are fully present to the moment in your breath and you can interact with others and situations that arise rather than react—remember you are "Response-able". You are in charge of your self. No one else is. As Eleanor Roosevelt said, "No one can make you feel inferior without your consent."

Many people feel that they do not have control over their beliefs and thoughts. They let circumstances influence their lives, which is condition-based living. But you have control as indicated above. You can control what you believe and your actions and reactions in relation to circumstances. So what do you choose today? To pause throughout the day engaging the APB of awareness and harmonic breath to refocus

---

15 Siegel, Dan, *The Pocket Guide to Interpersonal Neurobiology*, W.W. Norton & Company, 2012

16 Murphy, Joseph. *Think Yourself to Health, Wealth & Happiness*, Prentice Hall Press, 2002, pg. 149

and ensure your thoughts are in alignment with your desire—or will you let fear, anxiety, and dis-ease rule your life?

Choose to have inner peace to enable you to imagine and believe the life you desire filled with abundant wealth, vibrant health, harmonic relationships, inspiring work, and ultimate success by creating harmony within.

Prayer and Meditation

The purpose of all prayer and meditation is interior silence. When we think of prayer we think we must be using words but that is not always the case. Yes there are prayers for others and for our own hopes that we express in words, yet there is a powerful connection that begins when we just remain present to the moment and bring clear focus to the situation we find ourselves in with the people we are with.

There are many ways that you can find centered focus to calm your mind. Go for a walk. Lie on the ground and gaze up into the sky. Stand by a stream and focus on the rushing water, become one with its flow and sound. Sit by a waterfall and hear the healing laughter of the falling water. Take a walk on a beach or walk through a garden and allow your mind to calm and fall silent just being in the presence of nature. Everything can be an invitation to mindfulness by being fully present to the activity in which you are engaged. You can focus on a verse of poetry, listen closely to music, observe art or anything on which you can focus and feel joy, relief, and love.

Use of a Mantra—a mantra is that which focuses and protects the mind from distraction and negativity and can transform your energy, breath, and mind. I use a single word and repeat it again and again so that when my mind tries to run off with me, I can bring it back to focus and calm. I often just repeat—peace, peace, peace.

This helps you focus the mind and breath rather than letting it run away with you like a runaway team of horses that I used as an example earlier. This does not have to be overly solemn. It can be joyful and engage happiness and ease within the mind, body, and soul. It is not meant to feel forced, or cause anxiety, or create dis-ease but to gently add focus to your being. It is not about striving for perfection. We are human and the mind will certainly be drawn to thoughts and emotions. Just observe the thoughts that enter your mind and let them flow and go. Try not to overreact or be hard on yourself. Ordering yourself to "pay attention" will not get you anywhere. Gently bring your awareness back by focusing on your breath and letting the mantra flow.

Begin practicing in short sessions. Just focus on the breath for one minute even, but do this often throughout the day. It is by sensing the APB as described earlier—the awareness that you are becoming tense then start to focus on the breath. Release the negative thoughts that may be racing through your mind and say your mantra with your breath. It is the purpose of this meditative practice to bring your awareness and focus into everyday life not just when you have the perfect meditative environment. It is meant to offer peace, relief, and hope to every moment, which takes mindfulness and purposefully connecting yourself to your awareness.

This awareness can be enhanced by linking it to an activity such as keeping focused on what you are eating rather than just gulping your food. It can be used to enhance your presence to every activity that you complete. The more often you bring this focus to everyday life, the more easily you will engage this practice in times of rising emotions, as your physical body begins to tense or when your thoughts become fixed on negative, self-defeating, and deprecating messages within your mind.

MESSAGE 6

*Malachi has shared with me that I
should shut the TV off and ignore CNN*

he Constantly Negative News as Mary Morrissay refers to it!
Unease, anxiety, tension, stress, and worry are all forms of fear
that we as humans experience by too much future and not
enough presence. Horses don't worry about the past or obsessively fear
the future. They only think in the now.

Prior to television and the Internet, we would not know of the
disasters, wars, and terrorism that haunt our dreams at night. It would
take weeks, months, or years to know of the devastation that may invade
another community or country. We now know of (selected) news from
around the world the moment it happens whereas previously we did
not. For some the evening news is of no consequence. It is happening to
"them" not me. Yet as I watched earthquakes, floods, war, malnourished
children, murders, and other attacks upon humanity I would retch
(strong word I know—but it made me nauseous!)

One evening when I was away Megan and Doug were watching
"Criminal Minds." Doug said it was quite disturbing so he suggested
that they change the channel to which Megan queried "Why?" Doug

said that if I were home that I would be very disturbed and upset by the show and would likely shut off the TV or at least changed the channel. Megan said it didn't bother her, to which Doug replied, "Well it should."

We have become immune to violence, aggression, poverty, and the struggles of others as they experience challenges and hardships that are caused by government/political oppression, greed, prejudices, or lack of compassion. I am not pointing fingers here. I have had to turn to children's commercials to find a channel less likely to cause me to feel uncomfortable and accountable. Does this mean we should do without? Do the scriptures tell us that we should live in poverty if our fellow humans do? I do not believe that the "narrow gate" is meant to encourage us to the same struggles but to reach within ourselves to find the balance of comforts and care and to do our best to serve others as we can. Does that always come around to the almighty buck? I do not believe so if we are willing and able to serve, to extend a hand, to help in more personal ways than our wallets can extend.

It is not for us to judge how others lead their lives or how much they contribute. It is for us to shed light upon and lift up our fellow travelers in this journey called life. It certainly is not an easy one. Each of us has our own challenges which may be little to some, huge to others, and to ourselves a doorway into awareness.

Jesus encourages us to "take the log out of our own eye to see the splinter in another." Let us not criticize, compare, or condemn another. As my mother would quip, "Do not throw stones from glass houses." Truly what goes around comes around. Perhaps slower and more laboriously than we think it should, but it does. Do not for a second believe that those who should cause injury to another are not somehow experiencing loneliness, anxiety, and fear. It is for the Lord to judge not us.

Please do not misunderstand that I feel individuals who cause suffering should not be incarcerated in this life. Yet letting go is not easy considering some of the atrocities that are caused by others, is the only way to find peace, joy, and harmony within again. It is something that we all must work at day by day. Alcoholics Anonymous has it right—"one day at a time" for everything. And truly it is one moment at a time. For if you find yourself in paradise it wouldn't be long before your mind would say "yes, but . . ." and negative thoughts, feelings, and beliefs may enter in again. It is moment by moment initiating the APB—Awareness of how you feel in your body when anxiety and negativity begin, Pause . . . ahhhhhhh, and breathe breathe breathe.

Jesus tells us do not worry about tomorrow for today has enough worries of its own and deal with those today. Don't let the mind travel so far ahead that you cannot cope with or enjoy this moment. As negativity rises up say, "hmmm, how interesting. I wonder what I will create in this?" It is about realizing that there are no problems—only situations to be dealt with now, or to be left alone and accepted as part of the "issues" of the present moment until they change or can be dealt with.

The mind unconsciously loves problems because it gives you an identity of sorts. Ask yourself is there joy, ease, and lightness in what I am doing? If there isn't then time is covering up the present moment and life is perceived as a burden or a struggle. But to *know* that you are *not* present is a great success: that knowing *is* presence. You can allow a challenge to awaken you, or you can allow it to pull you into even deeper sleep.

Strategies for a More Engaged Life

Turn off the television or avoid the shows that cause anxiety, worry, or are just devoid of any positive value. It does not mean that you do not care about what is going on in the world but reading or the Internet offer higher quality and accuracy.

Head out for a walk or do some type of exercise. Exercising can also improve your energy level and make you feel better overall. It will engage your body to produce endorphins (which are natural mood enhancers) and help reduce feelings of stress and anxiety. There are numerous advantages for your health and well-being so don't overcomplicate it— just put on a pair of running shoes and walk. Breathe deeply and put one foot in front of the other.

Walking is a great activity that increases blood circulation and oxygen to the brain, and will help to lower blood pressure. It helps to "clear your mind" and energize your body. Check with your doctor before trying anything new and always monitor how you are feeling and listen to your body as it guides you in your activity.

My exercise of choice is yoga. It helps keep my joints loosened up, and my back stretched. It also encourages me to breathe deep and long, which oxygenates the brain and encourages relaxation.

The important point here is to get off the couch, **turn off** the television, and be active!

- Take the dog for a walk.
- Ride a bike.
- Walk up a stairwell in your building at work.
- Park further away to get groceries.
- Join a fitness club if it helps you stay active.
- Ask a friend to walk with you! This will increase the chances of your success.
- Play catch with your son or daughter or kick a ball around.

It doesn't have to be a regimented workout program. Do what you love and enjoy doing it is the key to being active! Remember: If you are beginning any activity program it is important to check with your doctor to ensure it is right for you!

Play spontaneously—as I watch from my window I see the horses start running and playing for seemingly no reason at all. They are enjoying the being in the moment, experiencing the freedom and you can almost hear them laughing as they play and nip at each other—kicking, bucking, and running. Life does not have to be so serious! So find joy in your day, laugh, and relax and let go of the negative.

MESSAGE 7

Flow With Your Emotions

M alachi has taught me to flow with my emotions rather than smother them. When we are in the presence of the horses our emotions are "mirrored" by them back to us. They sense our fears, feel our anxieties, reflect our frustration and anger, and bring awareness to the sadness we are enveloped in. They can reveal to us when we are not being authentic or are wearing a "game face" i.e., experiencing one emotion and trying to cover it with another.

Daniel Goleman in *Emotional Intelligence* argues that the mind's intellect is far too narrow and builds a case for emotional intelligence such as qualities of self-awareness, motivation, altruism, and compassion. Emotional processes work faster than the mind, it takes a power stronger than the mind to bend perception, override emotional circuitry, and provide us with the intuitive feeling instead. Our emotions have also been found to profoundly affect our heart and its torus field, with positive emotions bringing coherence, and negative emotions incoherence.

Many times we have been taught by society to smother our emotions. We are embarrassed to cry, we don't get too excited, we push down our anger, and all sorts of guidelines that eventually cause an explosion of emotion. I heard Mary Morrissey explain that holding your emotion in is similar to holding a beach ball under the water, eventually you just can't hold it down anymore, your arms tire and the ball explodes out of your control.

Our emotions are the consequences of our experiences. Emotions are very powerful yet we can learn to flow and befriend them to always return to a sense of harmony with ease and flow. Emotions are neither good nor bad—they just are. They help us to release tension, maneuver through loss, express our concerns, show we care, and resonate with others to understand what they may be experiencing.

Plato compared emotions to wild horses that need to be tamed and reined in by the intellect. It is important to begin to sense and feel, and identify how the emotions begin and feel in our bodies before our emotions become runaway wild horses—before they are running amuck and you lose control.

To understand our emotions and the feelings behind them, we need to be sensitive to how our bodies indicate that a certain sense or emotion is rising. Again, emotions are neither good nor bad. It all depends on how you flow through and express them. You can be angry and ask yourself, "What boundary has been crossed? What has happened that I feel betrayed, taken advantage of, or perhaps not having my needs heard?"

It is really important to know how an emotion feels within your body. What happens when you become angry for instance? Again the horses helped me to sense this awareness as they mirrored my emotions and feelings within the round pen. I was angry one day, but denying it so I could show a participant an activity in the round pen, Malachi stayed clear of me. Yet when I was able to identify the emotion and acknowledge how I was feeling, he came to me to help me work through the feelings. I was able to breathe and pause to ask myself if I was feeling angry or frustrated?

Anger causes me to tense, purse my lips, squint my eyes, increase my respiration, and feel like a tiger about to pounce. I feel the emotion in the moment but it doesn't seem to last overlong for me or lead to unexpressed resentment. I become frustrated when I repeatedly try to accomplish some task but can't seem to get the desired results. My neck and back become tense. It is an ongoing feeling that doesn't spike like my anger, but smolders below the surface. By identifying how the two different emotions feel in my body, how I react to them and interact with others when I experience them, I could flow easier and question what I did to exacerbate them.

What was I doing that was frustrating me? What was it I had to do differently to release the feelings of frustrations? Was there someone that could give me feedback? Was there something I could do differently?

Making the connection between feeling and emotion is the key to expressing your needs in the moment. If you can sense the rise of feelings of anger in your body, then you will have a better chance of bringing awareness to the moment and what you really need rather than exploding or sacrificing relationships to strong emotions. It is felt that unexpressed emotion can lead to dis-ease or illnesses that reflect the long-term emotional pain you may be suppressing. Ongoing tension can cause chronic neck pain and perhaps back pain. Constant worry can wear upon your mind and can contribute or aggravate heart disease and other pathological states to make them worse.

It is also important to monitor emotions for a reflection of happiness in your life, to sense and feel better feeling emotions as often as you can rather than smothering them or letting them simmer below the surface. So creating time within your day to become aware of how you are feeling, what sensations you may be experiencing, and doing Harmonic Breathing three to four times per day is essential. With this awareness you can change the emotional resonance you may be feeling. Below is the "Compass of Emotional Resonance Gauge" that I have created to help you identify the different emotions you may be experiencing.

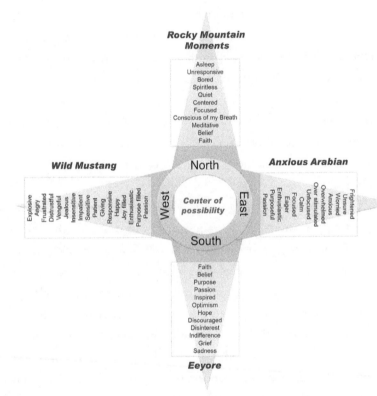

As you can see, at the far arms of the compass are emotions which may be creating dis-ease in your life. These emotions could be indications that you need to begin to take new actions in your life to make a change in direction and begin to move toward the center of the compass where you will find hope filled emotions that will create a life of ease, purpose, and love. Again, the emotion is neither good nor bad. It just is as it is.

It is meant to inform and help you to understand what is happening within and around you.

You cannot spontaneously move directly from sadness and grief to joy; your subconscious will deny that such a dramatic change is possible, especially if you have been feeling depression, sadness, or worry for a very long time. Or perhaps it is completely understandable in the midst of loss to feel grief, but if it is impairing your ability to cope over the long term, the feeling may be indicating that a pattern has begun that is impacting your life in ways detrimental to your wellbeing.

It is possible to connect consciously to the feeling and begin to feel even a bit of relief by choosing to move up the arm of the compass towards the centre to a better feeling emotion by just one move toward the centre of possibility. (Please however, if you feel deep depression, suicidal thoughts, or overwhelming dis-ease, it is important to seek medical guidance from your doctor, social worker, or other professionals who can assist you with dealing with your problems.)

At the hub of the compass is the place of possibility where you feel belief in self and others with a knowing within the mystery of life that grounds you and where you have the faith and courage to be authentic and the passion to live purposefully as you design it to be.

"Rocky Mountain Moments"

I chose the North as "Rocky Mountain Moments". These are peace filled, centered moments at the hub of the compass and further out those emotions and feelings that may cause dis-ease, distress, impairment of functioning and the inability to cope day-to-day. Although sleep is essential, if you are sleeping too much or are having difficulties sleeping this may indicate a need to be more attuned to the needs or your body, mind, and spirit.

Malachi is a Rocky Mountain horse. I used his breed to represent this arm of the "Emotional Compass" as they are typically quiet, calm, and grounded. Yet some would say too calm as many horses of this breed lack the quickness of response that an Arabian horse may have. To the North in many traditions the Elders, Horse Ancestors, and the presence of animal consciousness resides. It is the quiet calm mountainesque moments that are achieved by present moment focus of the horses and the wisdom of the sacred writings that can assist in bringing one to higher awareness and intuitive being.

This arm includes a variety of emotional states from one extreme of being unresponsive and perhaps dull to find a place of faith and the centre of possibility, which opens, draws, and attracts that which you desire.

Asleep	Focused
Unresponsive	Empowered
Bored	Conscious of my Breath
Disinterested	Freedom
Pessimism	Love
Spiritless	Positive Expectation
Powerlessness	Belief
Quiet	Centre of Possibilities
Centred	

If I attune to my body while I am in a Rocky Mountain moment I am relaxed, my mind is calm, I may be smiling and just enjoying myself. The APB is where the shift begins so that you have increased awareness to the need to change and you can choose to engage another emotion or feeling. I can't jump from boredom to conscious, focused awareness immediately but I can breathe in the quietude, become centered and then engage in the centre of possibilities. It is a process of awareness and choices to make, even slight movement on the arm of emotions on the compass. Awareness is the heart of all possibilities.

To the South, at the opposite end is Eeyore, the donkey from Winnie the Pooh. I chose him lovingly because we used to tease my husband that he was Eeyore. He now chooses to think in more positive life giving ways knowing that what you think and feel is what becomes your reality but at one time even if it was a glorious day he would assure us it was going to rain. If I thought of a great idea and was sharing this with him he immediately would come up with a million ways that it just wouldn't work.

It is hard being Eeyore and it doesn't feel good either. After my accident I found myself in, and still find it easy to slip into the Eeyore state of mind. To slide up the arm to a better feeling I have found that I need to surround myself with positive people with the same mindset and with positive and hope filled outlooks.

Emotion is contagious. The horses sense this all the time. Once one jumps or becomes frightened it will go through each horse to raise their heads, jump, or run. As my mother used to say, "If you lie with dogs you might get fleas," in other words, how you feel, emote, even think is influenced by those around you. So gravitate to those who are optimistic, hopeful, eager, full of appreciation, and inspired to make a difference for themselves and others to live a purposeful life full of positive opportunities. The emotion at the farthest end of the compass to the south is depression and coming closer to the centre we find hope, optimism, inspiration, and those of improved feeling, faith, and the centre of possibilities. Again, don't expect to move from sadness, grief, or feelings of unworthiness spontaneously. Encourage yourself to feel just a wee bit better in the moment to pause in awareness and breathe to choose to move up the arm of the Emotional Compass to a better feeling emotion and at least a wee bit of relief.

Sadness	Hope
Depression	Optimism
Grief	Eagerness
Guilt	Enthusiasm
Unworthiness	Appreciation
Indifference	Inspired
Disinterest	Faith
Discouraged	Centre of Possibility
Disappointment	

To the East is a feeling of anxiety and if you have ever watched an Arabian horse prance and step around a ring you could imagine where I get the visual idea that I have of an Anxious Arabian. Again not all Arabians are high-strung, excitable but in general terms let's say the Arabian is at a different level of vibration of Eeyore or my Rocky Mountain Moments.

If I am to the East I am anywhere from being afraid or paralyzed by fear and can bring awareness to the moment through the APB to choose to move closer to the centre of possibilities one feeling and emotion at a time.

Fear	Calm
Unsure	Focused
Doubt	Eager
Hopelessness	Enthusiastic
Worried	Hopeful
Anxious	Passion
Overwhelmed	Centre of Possibilities
Over stimulated	
Unfocused	
Impatient	

To the West we have the Wild Mustang Mind. Certainly not all mustangs are wild but they certainly love wild freedom more than they do being reined in if given the choice.

Nevertheless, I chose the Mustang to express the Wild Mind that which is

Explosive	Sensitive
Angry	Patient
Frustrated	Giving
Distrustful	Responsive
Vengeful	Happy
Blame	Joy filled
Jealous	Enthusiastic
Insensitive	Purposeful
Impatient	Centre of Possibilities

Now is this all clear cut in a row proceeding to the centre of possibilities? Each arm of the compass does not exist in exclusion. Inspect the compass and circle the emotions you may be experiencing and look at each of the emotional choices you can make to help you feel better in the present moment and experience even a little relief. Ease and joy can be reached step by step with patience and love. Love yourself as you journey to possibilities. I saw the word "Impossible" written on an overpass once but there was an apostrophe between the "I" and "M" changing it to I'M Possible—I'MPOSSIBLE!

It is your choice. It is possible. It is not weakness to ask for help or to see a counselor, specialist, or a horse to help you navigate through strong feelings and emotions. Ask yourself "What would I like to feel right now?" Then make the adjustment. Only you can do that. No one else can do it for you. Guidance and medical help may be essential and necessary, yet it is you who will have to take the steps.

No one can make you feel worthy or unworthy, to feel hope filled or disappointed, to experience joy and happiness, or anger and frustration. Once you begin to practice the APB frequently throughout your day you will notice when you are moving to a feeling that is better than your current feeling.

Nothing happens in isolation. There are all sorts of outside influences as I have highlighted such as CNN—Constantly Negative News, people experiencing challenges and sharing their dis-ease with you, your car will perhaps not start, you may drop a glass and break it but in that moment you must choose a better thought or feeling in response to outside influences. Will you lose your temper? Will you feel sad? Of course you will. For goodness sake, life is about experience, learning, and knowing that all is meant to help us to grow. Why would we have emotions if they were not meant to assist and direct us in our lives?

Strategies to lift your mood

Music – Music isn't just intellectual it is emotional and reflects our personalities. We listen to music to engage our emotions for excitement, joy, passion, and to lift us out of our current state to a more desirable state. Our heart sings when we listen to music. All of our senses are engaged.

Mikayla was part of a music group called the "Treble Makers." She sings beautifully and I love to hear her singing as she moves throughout the house. As a mom my heart soars when I hear her. Many times her group would go to nursing homes to sing and you could see the seniors become enlivened with joy as they listened. Even the ones that you knew were lost within their own minds would rouse when the music began. There is a universal need to listen to music that engages our emotions as the songs tell a story that we enter in and feel moved by. And it truly does move us! I cannot sit still when I hear a piece I love and that lifts our mood as we rock back and forth to the music.

In Dr. Amen's book, *Change Your Brain Change Your Life*, he states that singing in the shower can heal and enhance your temporal lobes and lift your mood. It doesn't matter if you are a rock star or not—it has been well supported that singing has healing qualities. Of course every kindergarten teacher knew this! If we sang while doing a task it was more fun, we remembered the steps easier and we were able to keep focused on the task much longer and we were much happier. And I have to admit—if I am overwhelmed with a task that I am doing on the computer or blocked when I am writing I click on Mozart in my iTunes library and I feel calmer, focused, and relaxed while it is playing in the background as I work. So sing along with your own favourite tunes or download Mozart and relax.

Movement—I have talked about exercise and movement previously but it is worth repeating. Once you have your doctor's OK, start to do activities you enjoy. Putting one foot in front of the other and strolling outside engages the senses of nature and endorphins, mood enhancers, are released to make you feel so much better. To increase your chances of continuing with a walking program or exercise ask a friend to join you. This increases your probability of success by making it fun and you have someone to encourage you and be accountable to, but always check with your doctor to ensure you are able to increase your physical movement.

Minding your Mood—Keep a journal of times of the day that you feel less enthusiastic, a loss of energy, or a time you feel little motivation. I find my difficult time to be in the evenings. I sit watching television with my family and I start to berate myself that I should be doing more than resting and enjoying a television show. I do think more activity with less television is the best approach but if you feel joy, peace, and contentment this way, then by all means do so. Find shows that are funny and light rather than always murder and mayhem with death and destruction. We don't think those things work their way into our well-being but the subconscious absorbs what it is fed and therefore, you may be retaining more of the negativity than you imagined. Time of inactivity such as television I believe should always be balanced by fresh air, exercise, and fun with friends. By keeping a journal you will become aware of the trends of times you tire and become agitated, short tempered, feel overwhelmed, or sad and can make the adjustment needed to improve your mood.

MESSAGE 8

Be okay with who you are and be authentic

Horses intuitively know if you are being authentic or not. I have watched numerous times as an individual walks into the round pen with a horse and is not truly present. They may be pretending that they are at ease and wanting to do the activity but the horses are never fooled by this act. One of our guests stood before Bill while I did a guided meditation for the group. The initial piece was done facing away from the horse and then I asked the group to turn and engage with the horse before them. When he looked around Bill was facing the back of the stall with his butt directly to the participant and the fellow said he looked around to him and Bill said to him "When you are truly ready to do this I will come to you." The fellow laughed and said to us later in the group that he really wasn't engaged in the exercise he was off thinking of other things and what he had to do when he got back to one of his own groups he was working with. He said however that when he took a breath and let Bill know that he was present and willing to engage in the activity, Bill turned directly to him and came nose to nose to share his breath and presence together. This was truly beautiful, authentic, and engaging in life with another sentient being.

I AM who I AM—I AM Limitless—My "I AM Limitless" logo expresses the very essence and precursor for happiness by Creating Harmony From Within! It all begins with the "I AM". Many people put an upside down horseshoe on the doorway to catch luck but it really isn't an occasional ringing of a horseshoe that brings you success! It all begins within to connect to the "I AM" harmony, vitality, happiness, and joy.

The whole advertising industry and consumer society would collapse if people became enlightened and no longer sought to find their identity through things but rather from within. The ego equates having with being. "I have therefore I am." Yet the more you seek happiness outside of yourself, the more contentment, happiness, and peace will elude you. Our newest technologies and toys only excite us for a time and then the cottage sits empty, the wave runners sit in the garage after a week of use, and the newest vehicle sits parked because you might scratch it if you take it out. We crave more speed, noise, gadgets, brain numbing TV, or a stimulating Wii game to cover our true feelings of sadness, loneliness, and lack of true connection with others and ourselves. Thomas Merton, an Anglo-American Catholic writer and mystic, wrote, *"We are so obsessed with doing that we have no time and no imagination left for being."*[17]

Many people never realize that there can be no "salvation" in anything they do, possess, or attain. It must come from within and then

---

17   Inchausti, Robert, The Pocket Thomas Merton, New Seeds Books, 300 Massachusetts. Ave, Boston, Massachusetts, 02115, 2005.

you will draw to you all of the possibilities you can dream of. You may gain outer riches and yet experience inner poverty or to "gain the world and lose your soul" as Jesus puts it. I am not saying that you cannot have beautiful things, a great car or a boat. Lord these things are grand and fun. Yet if all you do is work to put the gas in the boat or make the payments for the car, you are sure to become anxious, frustrated, and perhaps find very little time to enjoy your toys and perhaps you are sacrificing the greatest gifts in the world—your family and friends. This time cannot be replaced. This moment is really the most important one in your life to show you care, to reveal and feel who you truly are.

The ego really knows nothing of just being present and still, but believes that you will be saved by doing more. Your life becomes a race of lists, a race for time, losing our minds and peace in doing more frantically and losing yourself.

And so I come to Malachi's last message to me ...

Be still—I have always been one to "git 'r done" but now not so much. To be honest—I can't, at least not the things I used to do, but I live now in the moment, incredible moments when I am able to be still and breathe and soak in the sunsets, the full moons, the deer out in our fields.

One night when I went to fill the water tank Malachi met me at the gate as he usually does and he rested his head on my left shoulder and then gently and very slowly he lifted his head and put it on my right shoulder. He then leaned his neck to my ear and I could hear his heartbeat . . . his breath . . . and it felt like the very rhythm of life. It was a sacred time that if I had not fallen, if I had not slowed the pace of my life, I would have missed the very rhythm of life. What are you missing when you cannot be still, present, and aware? What might you become aware of if you paused in your day to catch one breath, to hear one heartbeat, and to feel the very breath of God.

Some things just have to be believed to be seen!

Truly, it is my faith that makes me strong. Over 300 times the Bible tells us "Do not worry," "Do not fear," "I am with you." No, I do not believe in an empty faith where everything is rainbows and sweet jellybeans. After being temporarily paralyzed from the waist down in my early 40s, experiencing a mini stroke and acquiring a brain injury, I'd be foolish to say that difficult circumstances never occur to those who have faith. Julian of Norwich wrote, "All is well and in all matter of things, all is well."[18] She believed that hope is viable even in the times of struggle and when God seems furthest away. As C.S. Lewis said, "God whispers in our pleasures and screams in our pain."[19]

Mikayla, wrote this on her mirror, which we share as a favorite quote taken from Nicolas Spark.

"I have faith that God will show you the answer. But you have to understand that sometimes it takes a while to be able to recognize what God wants you to do. That's how it often is. God's voice is usually nothing more than a whisper, and you have to listen very carefully to hear it. But other times, in those rarest of moments, the answer is obvious and rings as loud as a church bell."[20]

I know God has been ringing the bell strong and hard for me, "Wake up and smell the coffee and the roses; embrace your children; love your husband; appreciate your friends; and spend time in my garden of green grass, towering trees and with my precious animals. Be Still."

I would like to end this article with something called "The Testimony of a Confederate Soldier". I hear my own voice in this writing—perhaps this will resonate with you too.

---

18   Furlong, Monica, The Wisdom of Julian of Norwich, Lion Publishing, 255 Jefferson Ave. S.E. Grand Rapids, Michigan, U.S., 49503, 1996.

19   Lewis, C.S., A Grief Observed, bantam Book, 666 Fifth Ave., New York, NY, 10017, 1961

20   Sparks, Nicholas, The Last Song, Grand Central Publishing, Hachette Book Group, 237 Park Ave, New York, NY, 10017, 2009

I asked God for strength that I might achieve.

I was made weak that I might learn humbly to obey.

I asked for health that I might do greater things.

I was given infirmity that I might do better things.

I asked for riches that I might be happy.

I was given poverty that I might be wise.

I asked for power that I might have the praise of men.

I was given weakness that I might feel the need of God.

I asked for all things that I might enjoy life.

I was given life that I might enjoy all things.

I got nothing that I asked for—but everything I had hoped for.

Almost despite myself my unspoken prayers were answered.

I am among all people, most richly blessed.

—Author Unknown

Until next we meet again—Keep your dreams alive, your hopes high and your outlooks positive—rah jay urt! May the grace of God be with you!

About the Author

Sharon Campbell Rayment and her husband Doug care for Malachi and the rest of the horses at their Creating Harmony Within Ranch in Ontario, Canada. Their two daughters—Megan and Mikayla—are now off on their own great adventures.

Sharon holds a Bachelor of Science degree in nursing, a Master's degree in Divinity, founded the *Creating Harmony Within Ranch*, and is an international speaker. She and her herd of horses have helped hundreds of people overcome serious challenges in their lives. She is the author of *Creating Harmony From Within* and international bestselling co-author of the book, *Unwavering Strength.*

To become part of the "herd" and join Sharon and Malachi for "Weekly Wisdom Straight from the Horse's Mouth" visit www.creatingharmonywithin.com.

To contact Sharon to share her story with your group contact her at sharon@sharoncampbellrayment.com or visit sharoncampbellrayment.com

Bibliography

I've read so many excellent books and listened to so many motivational tapes and speakers that it's difficult to tell where my thoughts end and the inspiration of others begins. I'm not sure that I can take credit for any original thought within this book, and therefore, I would like to acknowledge the people and authors who have had the greatest impact on my life. I have truly absorbed their messages as an essential part of my being, which I feel is the highest form of flattery. My hope is that I've been able to impart awareness and insight to others in a unique way that may lead to enlightenment and happiness from within.

Amen, Dr., *Change Your Brain Change Your Life,* Harmony; Rev Exp
    edition (Nov. 3 2015)
Dyer, Wayne, *Excuses Be Gone,* Hay House, USA, 2010.
Furlong, Monica, *The Wisdom of Julian of Norwich*, Lion Publishing,
    255 Jefferson Ave. S.E. Grand Rapids, Michigan, U.S., 49503,
    1996.

Goddard, Neville *The Power of Awareness*, Pacific Publishing Studio, USA, 2012.

Hanson, Rick & Siegel, Dan, *Buddha's Brain,* New Harbinger Publications, 2009.

Inchausti, Robert, *The Pocket Thomas Merton*, New Seeds Books, 300 Massachusetts Ave, Boston, Massachusetts, 02115, 2005.

Lewis, C.S., *A Grief Observed*, Bantam Book, 666 Fifth Ave., New York, NY, 10017, 1961.

Murphy, Joseph. *Think Yourself to Health, Wealth & Happiness,* Prentice Hall Press, 2002.

Pearce Chilton Joseph, *The Heart-Mind Matrix,* 2012.

Siegel, Dan, *The Pocket Guide to Interpersonal Neurobiology,* W.W. Norton & Company, 2012.

Sparks, Nicholas, *The Last Song*, Grand Central Publishing, Hachette Book Group, 237 Park Ave, New York, NY, 10017, 2009.

The Holy Bible, The New Revised Standard Version, Oxford Press, Anglicized Edition, Oxford University Press 1998.

A free eBook edition is available with the purchase of this book.

To claim your free eBook edition:

1. Download the Shelfie app.
2. Write your name in uppser case in the box.
3. Use the Shelfie app to submit a photo.
4. Download your eBook to any device.

Shelfie

A **free** eBook edition is available
with the purchase of this print book.

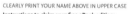

CLEARLY PRINT YOUR NAME ABOVE IN UPPER CASE

Instructions to claim your free eBook edition:
1. Download the Shelfie app for Android or iOS
2. Write your name in **UPPER CASE** above
3. Use the Shelfie app to submit a photo
4. Download your eBook to any device

Print & Digital Together Forever.

Snap a photo

Free eBook

Read anywhere

The Morgan James Speakers Group